Dismas Reinald Apostolis (Ed.)

Aakash (Tablet)

W0254630

Dismas Reinald Apostolis (Ed.)

Aakash (Tablet)

Tablet computer, Android (operating system), DataWind

Dic Press

Imprint

Permission is granted to copy, distribute and/or modify this document under the terms of the GNU Free Documentation License, Version 1.2 or any later version published by the Free Software Foundation; with no Invariant Sections, with the Front-Cover Texts, and with the Back- Cover Texts. A copy of the license is included in the section entitled "GNU Free Documentation License".

All parts of this book are extracted from Wikipedia, the free encyclopedia (www.wikipedia.org).

You can get detailed informations about the authors of this collection of articles at the end of this book. The editors (Ed.) of this book are no authors. They have not modified or extended the original texts.

Pictures published in this book can be under different licences than the GNU Free Documentation License. You can get detailed informations about the authors and licences of pictures at the end of this book.

The content of this book was generated collaboratively by volunteers. Please be advised that nothing found here has necessarily been reviewed by people with the expertise required to provide you with complete, accurate or reliable information. Some information in this book maybe misleading or wrong. The Publisher does not guarantee the validity of the information found here. If you need specific advice (f.e. in fields of medical, legal, financial, or risk management questions) please contact a professional who is licensed or knowledgeable in that area.

Any brand names and product names mentioned in this book are subject to trademark, brand or patent protection and are trademarks or registered trademarks of their respective holders. The use of brand names, product names, common names, trade names, product descriptions etc. even without a particular marking in this works is in no way to be construed to mean that such names may be regarded as unrestricted in respect of trademark and brand protection legislation and could thus be used by anyone.

Cover image: www.ingimage.com
Concerning the licence of the cover image please contact ingimage.

Publisher:
Dic Press is a trademark of
International Book Market Service Ltd., 17 Rue Meldrum, Beau Bassin, 1713-01 Mauritius
Email: info@bookmarketservice.com
Website: www.bookmarketservice.com

Published in 2012

Printed in: U.S.A., U.K., Germany. This book was not produced in Mauritius.

ISBN: 978-620-0-72014-6

Contents

Articles

References

Aakash_(tablet)

The initial release of the Aakash tablet.

Developer	DataWind
Manufacturer	DataWind
Type	Tablet computer
Introductory price	US$35 / ₹ 2,250
Operating system	Android 2.3
Power	2100 mAh li-po battery, 2-3 hr life
CPU	Cortex A8-700 MHz processor
Storage capacity	Flash memory Internal: 2 GB flash External: 2 to 32 GB microSD slot
Memory	256 MB RAM
Display	800 × 480 px 7 in (**unknown operator: u'strong'** cm) diagonal
Sound	Built in microphone; stereo earphones; 3.5mm jack
Input	Multi-touch resistive touchscreen, headset controls
Camera	None
Connectivity	Wi-Fi (802.11 a/b/g/n)
Online services	GetJar Market
Dimensions	190.5 mm (**unknown operator: u'strong'** in) H 118.5 mm (**unknown operator: u'strong'** in) W 15.7 mm (**unknown operator: u'strong'** in) D
Weight	350 g (**unknown operator: u'strong'** oz)
Website	[www.ubislate.com www.ubislate.com] [www.akashtablet.com www.akashtablet.com]

The **Aakash** is an Android-based tablet computer produced by British company DataWind.[1] It is manufactured by the India-based company Quad, at a new production centre in Hyderabad,[2] under a trial run of 100,000 units.[3] The tablet was officially launched as the *Aakash* in New Delhi on October 5, 2011. The Indian HRD ministry projects introduction of an upgraded second-generation model called Aakash 2 in April 2012.[4]

The Aakash is a low-cost tablet computer with a 7-inch touch screen, ARM 11 processor and 256 MB RAM[5] running under the Android 2.2 operating system. It has two universal serial bus (USB) ports[3] and delivers high definition (HD) quality video.[5] For applications, the Aakash will have access to Getjar, an independent market, rather than the Android Market.[6]

[3] The device was developed as part of the country's aim to link 25,000 colleges and 400 universities in an e-learning program.[7] Originally projected as a "$35 laptop",[8] the device will be sold to the Government of India at US$50[3] until further orders are received to obtain the $35 committed price, and will be distributed to university students for free. A commercial version of Aakash is currently marketed as *UbiSlate* 7+[9] at a price of $60.[10]

The Ubislate website accessed 2012-02-07 informs that a lakh Ubislate 7+ devices are being pre-booked each day, bookings are being taken for March, capacity for February being sold.[11]

Etymology

The device was initially called the *Sakshat* tablet, later changed to *Aakash*, which is derived from the Sanskrit word *Akasha* (Devanagari आका) with several related meanings, aether, empty space, and outer space. The word in Hindi means "sky".[5] [12]

History

Aspiration to create a "Made in India" computer was first reflected in a prototype "Simputer" that went into production in a small way. Bangalore based CPSU, Bharat Electronics Ltd manufactured around 5,000 Simputers to Indian Customers during 2002-07. In 2011, Kapil Sibal announced an anticipated low-cost computing device to compete with the One Laptop per Child (OLPC), though intended for urban college students rather than the OLPC's rural, underprivileged students

A year later, the MHRD announced that the low cost computer would be launched in 6 weeks. Nine weeks later the MHRD showcased a tablet named "Aakash", not nearly what had been projected and at US$60 rather than the projected $35. "NDTV" reported that the new low cost tablet was not a patch that was shown as a prototype and was going to cost about twice as much.[13]

While it was once projected as a laptop computer, the design has evolved into a tablet computer. At the inauguration of the national Mission on Education Programme organized by the Union HRD Ministry in 2009, joint secretary N. K. Sinha had said that the computing device is 10 inches (which is around 25.5 cm) long and 5 inches (12.5 cm) wide and priced at around $30.[14]

India's Human Resource Development Minister, Kapil Sibal unveiled a prototype on 22 July 2010. The price of the device exhibited was projected at $35, eventually to drop to $20 and ultimately to $10.[7] [15] [16] After the device was unveiled, OLPC Chairman Nicholas Negroponte offered full access to OLPC technology at no cost to the Indian team.[17]

Doubts about the tablet were dismissed in a television program "Gadget Guru" aired on NDTV in August 2010,[18] when it was shown to have 256 MB RAM and 2 GB of internal flash-memory storage and demonstrated running the Android operating system featuring video playback, internal Wi-Fi and cellular data via an external 3G modem.[19]

Specifications

As released on 5 October 2011, the Aakash features an overall size of 190.5 x 118.5 x 15.7 mm with a 180 millimetres (**unknown operator: u'strong'** in) resistive touchscreen,[20] a weight of 350 grams (**unknown operator: u'strong'** oz) and using the Android 2.2 operating system with access to the proprietary marketplace Getjar (not the Android Market), developed by DataWind.

The processor runs at 366 MHz; there is a graphics accelerator and HD video coprocessor. The tablet has 256 MB RAM, a micro SD slot with a 2 GB Micro SD card (expandable to 32 GB), two USB ports, a 3.5 mm audio output and input jack, a 2100 mAh battery, Wi-fi capability, a browser developed by DataWind, and an internal cellular and Subscriber Identity Module (SIM) modem. Power consumption is 2 watts, and there is a solar charging option.

The Aakash is designed to support various document (DOC, DOCX, PPT, PPTX, XLS, XLSX, ODT, ODP,PDF), image (PNG, JPG, BMP and GIF), audio (MP3, AAC, AC3, WAV, WMA) and video (MPEG2, MPEG4, AVI, FLV) file formats and includes an application for access to YouTube video content.[7] [18] [21] [22] [23] [24]

Specifications	Aakash	UbiSlate 7+
Price	₹ 2,500	₹ 2,999
Central processor unit speed	ARM11, 366 MHz	ARM Cortex-A8, 700 MHz
Random-access memory	256 MB	256 MB[25]
Battery	2100 mAh	3200 mAh
Operating system	Android 2.2 Froyo	Android 2.3 Gingerbread
Network	Wi-Fi	Wi-Fi + GPRS phone network
Phone Call	No	yes
Screen	Resistive	Resistive
App Store [26]	GetJar	Android Market
Made in	India	India

will have a micro-SD slot, and a 2 GB micro-SD flash memory card, upgradable to 32 GB, to store user data and programs not run from ROM. In Android 2.3 some applications and data can be moved from the ROM to the memory card.

Memory: ROM size has apparently not been stated by Datawind, but is estimated to be either 256 MB or 2 GB.[27] Both tablets have graphics processing cards, but the graphics memory size and GPU speed have not been stated .

Google Android Market: Aakash has no SIM card and insufficient processing power to use Google's Android Market, and will instead use the GetJar Marketplace. UbiSlate-7+ also will not have access to Google's Android Market confirmed by Google.

Network: Aakash supports wireless local area network (wireless LAN, Wi-Fi). It does not support GPRS/3G cellular networks. UbiSlate-7+ has GPRS Internet connection, a 2.5 generation Internet connection. Both tablets support an external 3G USB modem.

Browser

Datawind announced that their browser will use data compression technology to speed up data transmission. Compressed data such as ZIP files, JPEG images, MP3 audio, MPEG video will be transmitted at the basic speed, while uncompressed data will transmit typically at speeds up to 6 times faster, depending upon its nature. If and when successfully combined with Server-side web compression, 1G Analog Internet service might actually be able to compete with 2G or 3G digital internet service. Datawind claims that their browser can give up to 30 times faster speeds.[28]

[15] "Why India's $35 computer joke isn't funny" (http://economictimes.indiatimes.com/Hardware/articleshow/6214029.cms). *The Economic Times* (New Dehli). 25 July 2010. . Retrieved 25 July 2010.

[16] PIB Press Release (http://pib.nic.in/release/release.asp?relid=63417) PIB Retrieved 26 July 2010

[17] "OLPC's Negroponte supports India's $35 tablet concept" (http://www.siliconindia.com/shownews/OLPCs_Negroponte_supports_Indias_35_tablet_concept-nid-70313.html). 9 August 2010. . Retrieved 14 August 2010.

[18] NDTV Gadget Guru (http://www.ndtv.com/news/videos/video_player.php?id=157534) Gadget Guru exclusive: $35 laptop is here. Retrieved 13 August 2010

[19] "Aakash: World's Cheapest Tablet is here" (http://techtouche.com/worlds-cheapest-tablet-is-here). 5 October 2011. . Retrieved 5 October 2011

[20] http://venturebeat.com/2011/10/26/aakash-android-tablet-exclusive/

[21] "UbiSurfer Browser of India's Aakash Android Tablet" (http://browserfame.com/289/ubisurfer-browser-aakash-india-tablet-android) Gary, Mark. .

[22] "India's $35 tablet is here, for real. Called Aakash, costs $60" (http://www.engadget.com/2011/10/05/indias-35-tablet-is-here-for-real-called-aakash-costs-60/). Engadget. . Retrieved 2011-10-05

[23] "Aakash Tablet Hands On Review" (http://www.hungrynfoolish.com/2011/10/06/aakash-tablet-product-review-specs-pics-price-and-insights-from-the-maker-himself/). Hungry N Foolish. . Retrieved 2011-10-06.

[24] Halliday, Josh (23 July 2010). "India unveils cheapest laptop" (http://www.guardian.co.uk/world/2010/jul/23/india-unveils-cheapest-laptop). London: The Guardian. . Retrieved 25 July 2010.

[25] "Aakash Tablet: UbiSlate Netbook: Datawind Ubislate" (http://www.ubislate.com/specifications.html). *UbiSlate*. Datawind.com. Retrieved 2012-01-11.

[26] "Aakash Tablet Faqs" (http://www.ubislate.com/faqs.html). *UbiSlate7+*. Datawind.com. . Retrieved 2012-02-09.

[27] 2 GB internal flash memory in the specification could be the ROM.

[28] Datawind press release (http://datawind.com/pressrelease.html)

[29] Guardin-India untiels cheapest laptop (http://www.guardian.co.uk/world/2010/jul/23/india-unveils-cheapest-laptop) Retrieved 25 July 2010

[30] Harsimran Julka & Gulveen Aulakh. "Tender for $35 laptop project cancelled" (http://economictimes.indiatimes.com/tech/hardware/tender-for-35-laptop-project-cancelled/articleshow/7316466.cms). *The Economic Times*, ET Bureau 18 Jan 2011. News clipping by Pragadeesh Sekar on public interest

[31] "HRD press release" (http://pib.nic.in/newsite/erelease.aspx?relid=72584). . Retrieved December 30, 2011.

[32] "News Article about launch" (http://www.pluggd.in/35-laptop-launch-date-297). Pluggd.in. . Retrieved December 30, 2011.

[33] "Aakash Tablet's commercial variant in November" (http://www.hindustantimes.com/Akash-tablet-s-commercial-variant-in-November/Article1-754092.aspx). Hindustan Times. . Retrieved December 30, 2011.

[34] "Develop apps for Aakash, get rewarded" (http://m.timesofindia.com/PDATOI/articleshow/10915029.cms). Times of India. . Retrieved December 30, 2011

[35] http://www.sakshat.ac.in/

[36] Chauhan, Chetan (November 3, 2011). "Better, faster Aakash-2 to be launched in Feb 2012" (http://www.hindustantimes.com/technology/PersonalTech-Updates/Better-faster-Aakash-2-to-be-launched-in-Feb-2012/SP-Article1-764394.aspx). Hindustan Times, New Delhi.

[37] "Why India's Cheap Tablet May Not Work Out" (http://pcquest.ciol.com/content/editorscolumn/2011/111103102.asp). October 31, 2011. . The cheapest mobile handset doesn't compromise on the basics: calls, SMS, battery life. Nor does the Tata Nano. The Aakash does

[38] "World's cheapest tablet Aakash goes on sale for Rs 2500 Online with One week Delivery- www.aakashtablet.com" (http://www.skoolboyz.in/2011/12/worlds-cheapest-tablet-aakash-goes-on.html). . Retrieved 17 December 2011.

[39] "World's Cheapest Tablet - Aakash sold out" (http://www.skoolboyz.in/2011/12/worlds-cheapest-tablet-aakash-sold-out.html). . Retrieved 19 December 2011.

[40] Ubislate official website, Retrieved December 31, 2011.

[41] "1.4 million orders for world's cheapest tablet in India" (http://www.google.com/hostednews/afp/article/ALeqM5hIKVGIAbegcoKZJ7UCkQmmBtLPKg). AFP. 3 January 2012. . Retrieved 4 January 2012.

[42] "Upgraded version of UBISlate" (http://www.techteria.com/featured/aakash-worlds-cheapest-tablet-worth-buying/75). TechTeria. . Retrieved January 4, 2012.

[43] "Better Faster Aakash 2 to be launched in Feb 2012" (http://www.hindustantimes.com/technology/PersonalTech-Updates/Better-faster-Aakash-2-to-be-launched-in-Feb-2012/SP-Article1-764394.aspx). Hindustan Times. . Retrieved December 30, 2011.

[44] "Aakash Tablet Review" (http://indiatoday.intoday.in/story/aakash-tablet-review/1/164487.html). InToday. . Retrieved December 30, 2011.

[45] "RIL to Hit Data Services Market with 4G Technology on RS. 3500 Tablet" (http://reliance-industries.com/2011/12/ril-to-hit-data-services-market-with-4g-technology-on-rs-3500-tablet/). Reliance Industries. . Retrieved December 30, 2011.

[46] "Datawind,RIL talk on Chepaset Tab" (http://www.business-standard.com/india/news/datawind-ril-talkcheapest-tab/453933/) Business-Standard. . Retrieved December 30, 2011.

[47] (http://www.hindustantimes.com/India-news/NewDelhi/Aakash-2-can-cost-US-100-following-IIT-Rajasthan-recommendations/Article1-808649.aspx)

[48] (http://truthdive.com/2012/02/03/aakash-tablet-3-more-iits-to-work-for-making-it-cheaper.html)
[49] Clouds of doubt over Aakash (http://www.mydigitalfc.com/op-ed/clouds-doubt-over-aakash-680)

External links

- Official website (http://www.akashtablet.com)
- Official discussion forum (http://lcadforum.sakshat.ac.in/)
- Virtual Labs (http://vlabs.co.in/) (part of the Aakash project)
- Official website: DataWind (http://www.datawind.com/)
- Official website: Ubislate (http://www.ubislate.com/)

Android_(operating_system)

Home screen displayed by Samsung Galaxy Nexus, running Android 4.0 "Ice Cream Sandwich"

Company / developer	Google Inc, Open Handset Alliance
Programmed in	C (core),[1] Java (UI), C++
Working state	Current
Source model	Open Source[2] [3]
Initial release	20 September 2008
Latest stable release	4.0.4 (Ice Cream Sandwich) / 31 January 2012[4]
Package manager	Android Market / APK
Supported platforms	ARM, MIPS,[5] x86[6] [7]
Kernel type	Monolithic (Linux kernel)
Default user interface	Graphical
License	Apache License 2.0 Linux kernel patches under GNU GPL v2[8]
Official website	www.android.com [9]

Android is a Linux-based operating system for mobile devices such as smartphones and tablet computers. It is developed by the Open Handset Alliance led by Google.[10] [11]

Google purchased the initial developer of the software, Android Inc., in 2005.[12] The unveiling of the Android distribution in 2007 was announced with the founding of the Open Handset Alliance, a consortium of 86 hardware, software, and telecommunication companies devoted to advancing open standards for mobile devices.[13] [14] [15] [16] Google releases the Android code as open-source, under the Apache License.[17] The Android Open Source Project (AOSP) is tasked with the maintenance and further development of Android.[18]

Android has a large community of developers writing applications ("apps") that extend the functionality of the devices. Developers write primarily in a customized version of Java.[19] Apps can be downloaded from third-party sites or through online stores such as Android Market, the app store run by Google. As of October 2011 there were more than 400,000 apps available for Android, and the estimated number of applications downloaded from the

Android Market as of December 2011 exceeded 10 billion.[20] [21]

Android was listed as the best-selling smartphone platform worldwide in Q4 2010 by Canalys[22] [23] with over 200 million Android devices in use by November 2011.[24] According to Google's Andy Rubin, as of December 2011 there are over 700,000 Android devices activated every day.[25]

History

Foundation

Android, Inc. was founded in Palo Alto, California, United States in October, 2003 by Andy Rubin (co-founder of Danger),[26] Rich Miner (co-founder of Wildfire Communications, Inc.),[27] Nick Sears (once VP at T-Mobile),[28] and Chris White (headed design and interface development at WebTV)[29] to develop, in Rubin's words "...smarter mobile devices that are more aware of its owner's location and preferences".[29] Despite the obvious past accomplishments of the founders and early employees, Android Inc. operated secretly, revealing only that it was working on software for mobile phones.[29] That same year, Rubin ran out of money. Steve Perlman, a close friend of Rubin, brought him $10,000 in cash in an envelope and refused a stake in the company.[30]

Acquisition by Google

Google acquired Android Inc. on August 17, 2005, making Android Inc. a wholly owned subsidiary of Google Inc. Key employees of Android Inc., including Andy Rubin, Rich Miner and Chris White, stayed at the company after the acquisition.[12] Not much was known about Android Inc. at the time of the acquisition, but many assumed that Google was planning to enter the mobile phone market with this move.[12]

Post-acquisition development

At Google, the team led by Rubin developed a mobile device platform powered by the Linux kernel. Google marketed the platform to handset makers and carriers on the promise of providing a flexible, upgradable system. Google had lined up a series of hardware component and software partners and signaled to carriers that it was open to various degrees of cooperation on their part.[31] [32] [33]

Speculation about Google's intention to enter the mobile communications market continued to build through December 2006.[34] Reports from the BBC and *The Wall Street Journal* noted that Google wanted its search and applications on mobile phones and it was working hard to deliver that. Print and online media outlets soon reported rumors that Google was developing a Google-branded handset. Some speculated that as Google was defining technical specifications, it was showing prototypes to cell phone manufacturers and network operators.

In September 2007, *InformationWeek* covered an Evalueserve study reporting that Google had filed several patent applications in the area of mobile telephony.[35] [36]

Open Handset Alliance

On November 5, 2007, the Open Handset Alliance, a consortium of several companies which include Broadcom Corporation, Google, HTC, Intel, LG, Marvell Technology Group, Motorola, Nvidia, Qualcomm, Samsung Electronics, Sprint Nextel, T-Mobile and Texas Instruments unveiled itself. The goal of the Open Handset Alliance is to develop open standards for mobile devices.[15] On the same day, the Open Handset Alliance also unveiled their first product, Android, a mobile device platform built on the Linux kernel version 2.6.[15]

On December 9, 2008, 14 new members joined, including ARM Holdings, Atheros Communications, Asustek Computer Inc, Garmin Ltd, Huawei Technologies, PacketVideo, Softbank, Sony Ericsson, Toshiba Corp, and Vodafone Group Plc.[37] [38]

Android Open Source Project

The Android Open Source Project (AOSP) [39] is led by Google, and is tasked with the maintenance and development of Android.[40] According to the project "The goal of the Android Open Source Project is to create a successful real-world product that improves the mobile experience for end users."[41] AOSP also maintains the *Android Compatibility Program*, defining an "Android compatible" device "as one that can run any application written by third-party developers using the Android SDK and NDK", to prevent incompatible Android implementations.[41] The compatibility program is also optional and free of charge, with the *Compatibility Test Suite* also free and open-source.[42]

Version history

Android has seen a number of updates since its original release, each fixing bugs and adding new features. Each version is named, in alphabetical order, after a dessert.[43]

Recent releases

- **2.3 Gingerbread** refined the user interface, improved the soft keyboard and copy/paste features, improved gaming performance, added SIP support (VoIP calls), and added support for Near Field Communication.[44]
- **3.0 Honeycomb** was a tablet-oriented[45] [46] [47] release which supports larger screen devices and introduces many new user interface features, support for multi-core processors, hardware acceleration for graphics[47] and full system encryption.[48] [49] The first device featuring this version, the Motorola Xoom tablet, went on sale in February 2011.[50] [51]
  - **3.1 Honeycomb**, released in May 2011, added support for extra input devices, USB host mode for transferring information directly from cameras and other devices, and the Google Movies and Books apps.[52]
  - **3.2 Honeycomb**, released in July 2011, added optimization for a broader range of screen sizes, new "zoom-to-fill" screen compatibility mode, loading media files directly from SD card, and an extended screen support API.[53] Huawei MediaPad is the first 7 inch tablet to use this version[54]
- **4.0 Ice Cream Sandwich**, announced on October 19, 2011, brought Honeycomb features to smartphones and added new features including facial recognition unlock, network data usage monitoring and control, unified social networking contacts, photography enhancements, offline email searching, app folders, and information sharing using NFC. Android 4.0.3 Ice Cream Sandwich is the latest Android version that is available to phones. The source code of Android 4.0.1 was released on November 14, 2011.[55]

Design

Android consists of a kernel based on the Linux kernel, with middleware, libraries and APIs written in C and application software running on an application framework which includes Java-compatible libraries based on Apache Harmony. Android uses the Dalvik virtual machine with just-in-time compilation to run Dalvik dex-code (Dalvik Executable), which is usually translated from Java bytecode.[56]

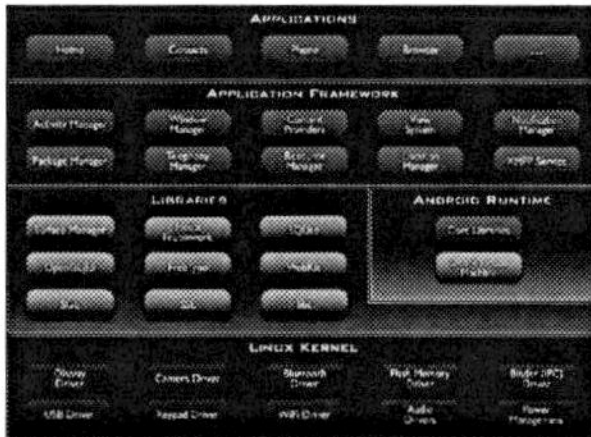

Architecture diagram

The main hardware platform for Android is the ARM architecture. There is support for x86 from the Android x86 project,[57] and Google TV uses a special x86 version of Android.

Linux

Android's kernel is based on the Linux kernel and has further architecture changes by Google outside the typical Linux kernel development cycle.[58] Android does not have a native X Window System nor does it support the full set of standard GNU libraries, and this makes it difficult to port existing Linux applications or libraries to Android.[59]

Certain features that Google contributed back to the Linux kernel, notably a power management feature called wakelocks, were rejected by mainline kernel developers, partly because kernel maintainers felt that Google did not show any intent to maintain their own code.[60] [61] [62] Even though Google announced in April 2010 that they would hire two employees to work with the Linux kernel community,[63] Greg Kroah-Hartman, the current Linux kernel maintainer for the -stable branch, said in December 2010 that he was concerned that Google was no longer trying to get their code changes included in mainstream Linux.[61] Some Google Android developers hinted that "the Android team was getting fed up with the process", because they were a small team and had more urgent work to do on Android.[64]

However, in September 2010, Linux kernel developer Rafael J. Wysocki added a patch that improved the mainline Linux wakeup events framework. He said that Android device drivers that use wakelocks can now be easily merged into mainline Linux, but that Android's opportunistic suspend features should not be included in the mainline kernel.[65] [66] In 2011 Linus Torvalds said that "eventually Android and Linux would come back to a common kernel, but it will probably not be for four to five years".[67]

In December 2011, Greg Kroah-Hartman announced the start of the Android Mainlining Project, which aims to put some Android drivers, patches and features back into the Linux kernel, starting in Linux 3.3.[68] further integration being expected for Linux Kernel 3.4.[69]

Features

Current features and specifications:[70] [71] [72]

Handset layouts

The platform is adaptable to larger, VGA, 2D graphics library, 3D graphics library based on OpenGL ES 2.0 specifications, and traditional smartphone layouts.

Storage

SQLite, a lightweight relational database, is used for data storage purposes.

Connectivity

Android supports connectivity technologies including GSM/EDGE, IDEN, CDMA, EV-DO, UMTS, Bluetooth, Wi-Fi, LTE, NFC and WiMAX.

Messaging

SMS and MMS are available forms of messaging, including threaded text messaging and now Android Cloud To Device Messaging (C2DM) is also a part of Android Push Messaging service.

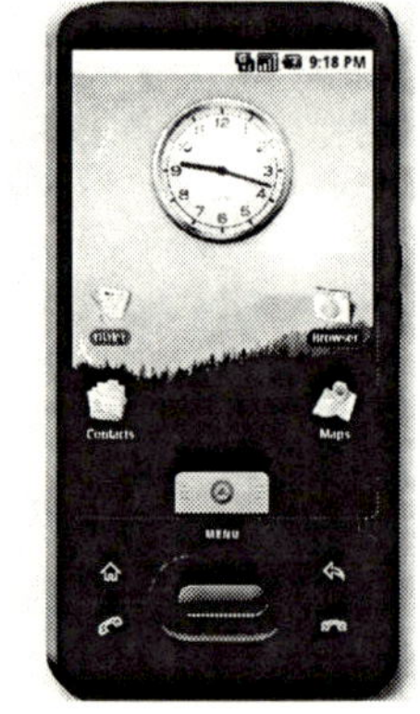

The Android Emulator default home screen (v1.5)

Multiple language support

Android supports multiple languages.[44]

Web browser

The web browser available in Android is based on the open-source WebKit layout engine, coupled with Chrome's V8 JavaScript engine. The browser scores 100/100 on the Acid3 test on Android 4.0.

Java support

While most Android applications are written in Java, there is no Java Virtual Machine in the platform and Java byte code is not executed. Java classes are compiled into Dalvik executables and run on Dalvik, a specialized virtual machine designed specifically for Android and optimized for battery-powered mobile devices with limited memory and CPU. J2ME support can be provided via third-party applications.

Media support

Android supports the following audio/video/still media formats: WebM, H.263, H.264 (in 3GP or MP4 container), MPEG-4 SP, AMR, AMR-WB (in 3GP container), AAC, HE-AAC (in MP4 or 3GP container), MP3, MIDI, Ogg Vorbis, FLAC, WAV, JPEG, PNG, GIF, BMP.[72]

Streaming media support

RTP/RTSP streaming (3GPP PSS, ISMA), HTML progressive download (HTML5 <video> tag). Adobe Flash Streaming (RTMP) and HTTP Dynamic Streaming are supported by the Flash plugin.[73] Apple HTTP Live Streaming is supported by RealPlayer for Android,[74] and by the operating system in Android 3.0 (Honeycomb).[47]

Additional hardware support

Android can use video/still cameras, touchscreens, GPS, accelerometers, gyroscopes, barometers, magnetometers, dedicated gaming controls, proximity and pressure sensors, thermometers, accelerated 2D bit blits (with hardware orientation, scaling, pixel format conversion) and accelerated 3D graphics.

Multi-touch

Android has native support for multi-touch which was initially made available in handsets such as the HTC Hero. The feature was originally disabled at the kernel level (possibly to avoid infringing Apple's patents on touch-screen technology at the time).[75] Google has since released an update for the Nexus One and the Motorola Droid which enables multi-touch natively.[76]

Bluetooth

Supports A2DP, AVRCP, sending files (OPP), accessing the phone book (PBAP), voice dialing and sending contacts between phones. Keyboard, mouse and joystick (HID) support is available in Android 3.1+, and in earlier versions through manufacturer customizations and third-party applications.[77]

Video calling

Android does not support native video calling, but some handsets have a customized version of the operating system that supports it, either via the UMTS network (like the Samsung Galaxy S) or over IP. Video calling through Google Talk is available in Android 2.3.4 and later. Gingerbread allows Nexus S to place Internet calls with a SIP account. This allows for enhanced VoIP dialing to other SIP accounts and even phone numbers. Skype 2.1 offers video calling in Android 2.3, including front camera support.

Multitasking

Multitasking of applications is available.[78]

Voice based features

Google search through voice has been available since initial release.[79] Voice actions for calling, texting, navigation, etc. are supported on Android 2.2 onwards.[80]

Tethering

Android supports tethering, which allows a phone to be used as a wireless/wired Wi-Fi hotspot. Before Android 2.2 this was supported by third-party applications or manufacturer customizations.[81]

Screen capture

Android supports capturing a screenshot by pressing the power and volume-down buttons at the same time.[82] Prior to Android 4.0, the only methods of capturing a screenshot were through manufacturer and third-party customizations or otherwise by using a PC connection (DDMS developer's tool). These alternative methods are still available with the latest Android.

External storage

Most Android devices include microSD slot and can read microSD cards formatted with FAT32, Ext3fs or Ext4fs file system. To allow use of high-capacity storage media such as USB flash drives and USB HDDs, many Android tablets also include USB 'A' receptacle. Storage formatted with FAT32 is handled by Linux Kernel VFAT driver, while 3rd party solutions are required to handle other popular file systems such as NTFS, HFS Plus and exFAT.

Uses

While Android is designed primarily for smartphones and tablets, the open and customizable nature of the operating system allows it to be used on other electronics, including laptops and netbooks, smartbooks,[83] [84] and ebook readers.[85] Further, Google intends to bring Android to televisions with Google TV, and the OS has seen niche applications on wristwatches,[86] headphones,[87] car CD and DVD players,[88] digital cameras,[89] portable media players[90] and landlines.[91]

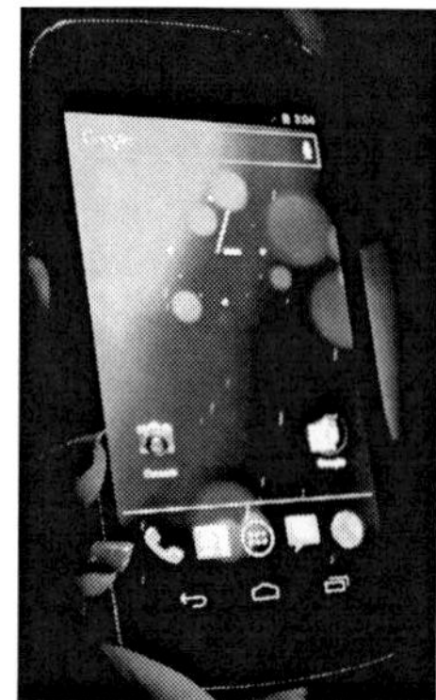

Galaxy Nexus, the latest "Google phone"

The first commercially available phone to run Android was the HTC Dream, released on 22 October 2008.[92] In early 2010 Google collaborated with HTC to launch its flagship[93] Android device, the Nexus One. This was followed later in 2010 with the Samsung-made Nexus S and in 2011 with the Galaxy Nexus.

iOS and Android 2.3.3 'Gingerbread' may be set up to dual boot on a jailbroken iPhone or iPod Touch with the help of OpeniBoot and iDroid.[94] [95]

In December 2011 it was announced the Pentagon has officially approved Android for use by its personnel.[96] [97] [98]

Google TV Home Screen

Applications

Applications are usually developed in the Java language using the Android Software Development Kit, but other development tools are available, including a Native Development Kit for applications or extensions in C or C++, Google App Inventor, a visual environment for novice programmers and various cross platform mobile web applications frameworks.

Android Market

The Android Market on a phone

Android Market is the online software store developed by Google for Android devices. An application program ("app") called "Market" is preinstalled on most Android devices and allows users to browse and download apps published by third-party developers, hosted on Android Market. As of October 2011 there were more than 300,000 apps available for Android, and the estimated number of applications downloaded from the Android Market as of December 2011 exceeded 10 billion.[20] [21] The operating system itself is installed on 130 million total devices.[99]

Only devices that comply with Google's compatibility requirements are allowed to preinstall Google's closed-source Android Market app and access the Market.[100] The Market filters the list of applications presented by the Market app to those that are compatible with the user's device, and developers may restrict their applications to particular carriers or countries for business reasons.[101]

Google has participated in the Android Market by offering several applications themselves, including Google Voice (for the Google Voice service), Sky Map (for watching stars), Finance (for their finance service), Maps Editor (for their MyMaps service), Places Directory (for their Local Search), Google Goggles that searches by image, Gesture Search (for using finger-written letters and numbers to search the contents of the phone), Google Translate, Google Shopper, Listen for podcasts and My Tracks, a jogging application. In August 2010, Google launched "Voice Actions for Android",[102] which allows users to search, write messages, and initiate calls by voice.

Alternatively, users can install apps directly onto the device if they have the application's APK file or from third party app stores such as the Amazon Appstore.[103]

Application security

An example of app permissions in Android Market.

Android applications run in a sandbox, an isolated area of the operating system that does not have access to the rest of the system's resources, unless access permissions are granted by the user when the application is installed. Before installing an application, Android Market displays all required permissions. A game may need to enable vibration, for example, but should not need to read messages or access the phonebook. After reviewing these permissions, the user can decide whether to install the application.[104]

Android has been criticized for providing an ineffective and too coarse grained permission system.[105] [106] In *Android Permissions Demystified*, Felt, Chin, Hanna, Song, and Wagner observe "... an install-time permission system is ineffective if developers routinely request more permissions than they require. Overprivileged applications expose users to unnecessary permission warnings and increase the impact of a bug or vulnerability." The authors then go on to survey overprivileged applications, including a Google authored reference implementations, using their Stowaway tool.[105] In *Dr. Android and Mr. Hide:*

Fine-grained security policies on unmodified Android, Jeon, Micinski, Vaughan, et. al. comment on the coarse grained permissions, stating "[the] deviation from least privilege increases the threat from vulnerabilities and malware. To address this issue, we present a novel system that can replace existing platform permissions with finer-grained ones."[106]

Some Android malware incidents have been reported involving rogue applications on Android Market. In August 2010, Kaspersky Lab reported detection of the first malicious program for Android, named Trojan-SMS.AndroidOS.FakePlayer.a, an SMS trojan which had already infected a number of devices.[107] In some cases applications which contained Trojans were hidden in pirated versions of legitimate apps.[108] [109] Google has responded by removing malicious apps from the Android Market, remotely disabling them on infected devices, and scanning newly-uploaded apps for potentially malicious software.[110] [111] Several security firms have released antivirus software for Android devices, in particular, AVG Technologies,[112] Avast!,[113] F-Secure,[114] Kaspersky,[115] McAfee[116] and Symantec.[117]

Privacy

Android smartphones have the ability to report the location of Wi-Fi access points, encountered as phone users move around, to build vast databases containing the physical locations of hundreds of millions of such access points. These databases form electronic maps to locate smartphones, allowing them to run apps like Foursquare, Latitude, Places, and to deliver location-based ads.[118]

Third party monitoring software such as TaintDroid,[119] an academic research-funded project, can, in some cases, detect when personal information is being sent from applications to remote servers.[120]

Marketing

The Android logo was designed along with the Droid font family made by Ascender Corporation.[121]

Android Green is the color of the Android Robot that represents the Android operating system. The print color is PMS 376C and the RGB color value in hexadecimal is #A4C639, as specified by the Android Brand Guidelines.[122] The custom typeface of Android is called Norad (cf. NORAD). It is only used in the text logo.[122]

Market share

Research company Canalys estimated in Q2 2009 that Android had a 2.8% share of worldwide smartphone shipments.[123] By Q4 2010 this had grown to 33% of the market, becoming the top-selling smartphone platform. This estimate includes the Tapas and OMS variants of Android.[22] By Q3 2011 Gartner estimates more than half (52.5%) of the smartphone market belongs to Android.[124]

In February 2010 ComScore said the Android platform had 9.0% of the U.S. smartphone market, as measured by current mobile subscribers. This figure was up from an earlier estimate of 5.2% in November 2009.[125] By the end of Q3 2010 Android's U.S. market share had grown to 21.4%.[126]

In May 2010, Android's first quarter U.S. sales surpassed that of the rival iPhone platform. According to a report by the NPD group, Android achieved 25% smartphone sales in the US market, up 8% from the December quarter. In the second quarter, Apple's iOS was up by 11%, indicating that Android is taking market share mainly from RIM, and still has to compete with heavy consumer demand for new competitor offerings.[127] Furthermore, analysts pointed to advantages that Android has as a multi-channel, multi-carrier OS.[128] In Q4 2010 Android had 59% of the total installed user base of Apple's iOS in the U.S. and 46% of the total installed user base of iOS in Europe.[129] [130]

As of June 2011, Google said that 550,000 new Android devices were being activated every day[131] — up from 400,000 per day a month earlier — and more than 100 million devices had been activated.[132] Android hit 300,000 activations per day back in December 2010. By July 14, 2011, 550,000 Android devices were being activated by Google each day, with 4.4% growth per week.[133] On 1 August 2011, Canalys estimated that Android had about

48% of the smartphone market share.[134] On October 13, 2011, Google announced that there were 190 million Android devices in the market.[135] As of November 16, 2011, during the Google Music announcement "These Go to Eleven", 200 million Android devices had been activated.[136] Based on this number, with 1.9% of Android devices being tablets, approximately 3.8 million Android Honeycomb Tablets have been sold.[137] On December 20, 2011. Andy Rubin announced that Google was activating 700,000 new Android devices daily.[25]

Usage share

Usage share of the different versions, by February 1, 2012.[138]

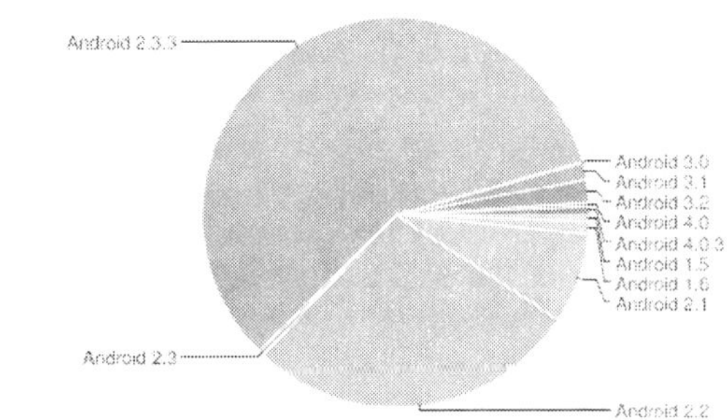

Usage share of the different versions, by February 1, 2012

Distribution	API level	%
4.0.x *Ice Cream Sandwich*	14-15	1.0%
3.x.x *Honeycomb*	11-13	3.4%
2.3.x *Gingerbread*	9-10	58.6%
2.2 *Froyo*	8	27.8%
2.0, 2.1 *Eclair*	7	7.6%
1.6 *Donut*	4	1.0%
1.5 *Cupcake*	3	0.6%

There were two more internal releases, called "Astro" and "Bender". The code names are in alphabetical order, and were allegedly changed from robots to desserts to avoid trademark issues.[139]

Retail stores

The carrier Telstra opened the world's first Android store, Androidland, on Bourke Street, Melbourne in December 2011.[140]

Intellectual property

Trademarks

In order to use the Android trademark, device manufacturers must ensure that the device complies with the Compatibility Definition Document (CDD) and then get permission from Google. Devices must also meet this definition to be eligible to license Google's closed-source applications, including the Android Market.[141] Participation in the compatibility program is free of charge.[42]

In September 2010, Skyhook Wireless filed a lawsuit against Google in which they alleged that Google had used the compatibility document to block Skyhook's mobile positioning service (XPS) from Motorola's Android mobile devices.[142] In December 2010 a judge denied Skyhook's motion for preliminary injunction, saying that Google had not closed off the possibility of accepting a revised version of Skyhook's XPS service, and that Motorola had terminated their contract with Skyhook because Skyhook wanted to disable Google's location data collection functions on Motorola's devices, which would have violated Motorola's obligations to Google and its carriers.[143]

Licensing

The source code for Android is available under free and open source software licenses. Google published their Linux kernel changes under the GNU General Public License version 2, and the rest of the code (including network and telephony stacks)[144] under the Apache License version 2.0.[145] [146] [147]

The Open Handset Alliance develops the GPL-licensed part of Android, that is their changes to the Linux kernel, in public, with source code publicly available at all times. The rest of Android is developed in private, with source code released publicly when a major new version is released. Typically Google collaborates with a hardware manufacturer to produce a flagship device (part of the Google Nexus series) featuring the new version of Android, then makes the source code available after that device has been released.[148]

In early 2011, Google chose to temporarily withhold the Android source code to the tablet-only Honeycomb release, creating doubts over Google's commitment to open source with Android.[149] The reason, according to Andy Rubin in an official Android blog post, was because Honeycomb was rushed for production of the Motorola Xoom,[150] and they did not want third parties creating a "really bad user experience" by attempting to put onto smartphones a version of Android intended for tablets.[151] The source code was once again made available in November 2011 with the release of Android 4.0.[152]

Patents

Both Android and Android phone manufacturers have been the target of numerous patent lawsuits. On 12 August 2010, Oracle sued Google over claimed infringement of copyrights and patents related to the Java programming language.[153] Specifically, the patent infringement claim references seven United States patents including US 5966702 [154], and US 6910205 [155] [156].

In response, Google submitted multiple lines of defense, counterclaiming that Android did not infringe on Oracle's patents or copyright, that Oracle's patents were invalid, and several other defenses. They said that Android is based on Apache Harmony, a clean room implementation of the Java class libraries, and an independently developed virtual machine called Dalvik.[157] [158] [159]

Microsoft has also sued several manufacturers of Android devices for patent infringement, and collects patent licensing fees from others. In October 2011 Microsoft said they had signed license agreements with ten Android device manufacturers, accounting for 55% of worldwide revenue for Android devices.[160] These include Samsung and HTC.[161]

Google has publicly expressed its dislike for the current patent landscape in the United States, accusing Apple, Oracle and Microsoft of trying to take down Android through patent litigation, rather than innovating and competing with better products and services.[162] In August 2011, Google started the process of purchasing Motorola Mobility for US$12.5 billion, which was viewed in part as a defensive measure to protect Android, since Motorola Mobility holds more than 17,000 patents.[163] In December 2011 Google acquired in the region of a thousand patents from IBM,[164] which may aid in defense against Oracle.[165] In February 2012, the U.S. Department of Justice and the European Union approved Google's aquisition of Motorola Mobility.[166]

See also

- CyanogenMod
- Google Android lawn statues
- Google Chrome OS
- Google Nexus
- List of Android devices
- Index of Android OS articles
- Rooting (Android OS)

References

[1] Lextrait, Vincent (November 2010). "The Programming Languages Beacon, v10.4" (http://www.lextrait.com/Vincent/implementations.html). . Retrieved 2012-02-20.

[2] "Philosophy and Goals | Android Open Source" (http://source.android.com/about/philosophy.html). Source.android.com. . Retrieved 2012-01-01

[3] "Codenames, Tags, and Build Numbers | Android Open Source" (http://source.android.com/source/build-numbers.html). source.android.com. . Retrieved 2012-02-21

[4] Xavier Ducrohet (December 16, 2011). "Android 4.0.3 Platform and Updated SDK tools" (http://android-developers.blogspot.com/2011/12/android-403-platform-and-updated-sdk.html). *Android Developers Blog*. . Retrieved 2012-02-20.

[5] "MIPS gets sweet with Honeycomb" (http://www.eetimes.com/electronics-news/4215490/MIPS-gets-sweet-with-Honeycomb). Eetimes.com. . Retrieved 2012-02-20.

[6] Mark LaPedus (April 26, 2011). "Porting Android to x86" (http://www.android-x86.org/). Android-x86. . Retrieved 2012-02-20

[7] Agam Shah (December 1, 2011). "Google's Android 4.0 ported to x86 processors" (http://www.computerworld.com/s/article/9222323/Google_s_Android_4.0_ported_to_x86_processors). Computerworld. . Retrieved 2012-02-20.

[8] "Licenses" (http://source.android.com/source/licenses.html). *Android Open Source Project*. Open Handset Alliance. . Retrieved 2012-02-20

[9] http://www.android.com/

[10] "Google Projects for Android" (http://www.webcitation.org/5wiw1JXa2). *code.google.com*. Google Inc. 2011. Archived from the original (http://code.google.com/android/) on 2011-02-23. . Retrieved 2012-02-20.

[11] "Philosophy and Goals" (http://www.webcitation.org/5wiy036ap). *source.android.com*. Google Inc. 2011. Archived from the original (http://source.android.com/about/philosophy.html) on 2011-02-23. . Retrieved 2012-02-20.

[12] Ben Elgin (August 17, 2005). "Google Buys Android for Its Mobile Arsenal" (http://www.webcitation.org/5wk7sIvVb). *businessweek.com*. Bloomberg L.P. Archived from the original (http://www.businessweek.com/technology/content/aug2005/tc20050817_0949_tc024.htm) on 2011-02-24. . Retrieved 2012-02-20.

[13] "Open Handset Alliance" (http://www.openhandsetalliance.com/). Open Handset Alliance. . Retrieved 2012-02-20.

[14] Jackson, Rob (December 10, 2008). "Sony Ericsson, HTC Androids Set For Summer 2009" (http://phandroid.com/2008/12/10/sony-ericsson-htc-androids-set-for-summer-2009/). *Android Phone Fans*. . Retrieved 2012-02-17.

[15] "Industry Leaders Announce Open Platform for Mobile Devices" (http://www.openhandsetalliance.com/press_110507.html) (Press release). Open Handset Alliance. November 5, 2007. . Retrieved 2012-02-17.

[16] "FAQ" (http://www.openhandsetalliance.com/oha_faq.html) (Press release). Open Handset Alliance. November 2007. . Retrieved 2012-02-20.

[17] "Android Overview" (http://www.openhandsetalliance.com/android_overview.html). Open Handset Alliance. . Retrieved 2012-02-15.

[18] "About the Android Open Source Project" (http://source.android.com/about/index.html). . Retrieved 2012-02-20.

[19] Shankland, Stephen (November 12, 2007). "Google's Android parts ways with Java industry group" (http://news.cnet.com/8301-13580_3-9815495-39.html). *CNET News*. . Retrieved 2012-02-15.

[20] Richard Wordsworth (October 23, 2011). "Android Market reaches 500,000 app mark" (http://www.t3.com/news/android-market-reaches-500000-app-mark). www.t3.com. . Retrieved 2012-02-20.

[21] Christina Bonnington (December 8, 2011). "Google's 10 Billion Android App Downloads: By the Numbers" (http://www.wired.com/gadgetlab/2011/12/10-billion-apps-detailed/). *wired.com*. . Retrieved 2012-02-15.

[22] Tarmo Virki and Sinead Carew (January 31, 2011). "Google topples Symbian from smartphones top spot" (http://uk.reuters.com/article/2011/01/31/oukin-uk-google-nokia-idUKTRE70U1YT20110131). *Reuters*. . Retrieved 2012-02-15.

[23] "Google's Android becomes the world's leading smart phone platform (Canalys research release: r2011013)" (http://www.canalys.com/newsroom/googleâs-android-becomes-worldâs-leading-smart-phone-platform). *Canalys*. January 31, 2011. . Retrieved 2012-02-15.

[24] Charles Arthur (October 14, 2011). "Mobile generating equivalent of $2.5bn a year, says Google chief" (http://www.guardian.co.uk/technology/2011/oct/14/android-google-ad-revenue). Guardian. . Retrieved 2012-02-20

[25] "Android Phones Pass 700,000 Activations Per Day, Approaching 250 Million Total" (http://techcrunch.com/2011/12/22/android-700000/). TechCrunch. December 22, 2011. . Retrieved 2012-02-15.

[26] Markoff, John (November 4, 2007). "I, Robot: The Man Behind the Google Phone" (http://www.nytimes.com/2007/11/04/technology/04google.html?_r=2&hp=&pagewanted=all). The New York Times. . Retrieved 2012-02-15.

[27] Kirsner, Scott (September 2, 2007). "Introducing the Google Phone" (http://web.archive.org/web/20100104054533/http://www.boston.com/business/technology/articles/2007/09/02/introducing_the_google_phone/). *The Boston Globe*. Archived from the original (http://www.boston.com/business/technology/articles/2007/09/02/introducing_the_google_phone/) on January 4, 2010. . Retrieved 2012-02-15.

[28] "T-Mobile Brings Unlimited Multiplayer Gaming to US Market with First Launch of Nokia N-Gage Game Deck" (http://newsroom.t-mobile.com/articles/t-mobile-nokia-N-Gage) (Press release). T-Mobile. September 23, 2003. . Retrieved 2012-02-15.

[29] Ben Elgin (August 17, 2005). "Google Buys Android for Its Mobile Arsenal" (http://www.webcitation.org/5wk7sIvVb). *businessweek.com*. Bloomberg L.P. Archived from the original (http://www.businessweek.com/technology/content/aug2005/tc20050817_0949_tc024.htm) on 2011-02-24. . Retrieved 2012-02-20. "In what could be a key move in its nascent wireless strategy, Google (GOOG) has quietly acquired startup Android Inc...."

[30] Vance, Ashlee (2011-08-07). "A Thousand Times Yes" (http://www.airsla.org/broadcasts/BusinessWeek110802.mp3). Bloomberg BusinessWeek. . Retrieved 2011-11-09.

[31] Block, Ryan (August 28, 2007). "Google is working on a mobile OS, and it's due out shortly" (http://www.engadget.com/2007/08/28/google-is-working-on-a-mobile-os-and-its-due-out-shortly). *Engadget*. . Retrieved 2012-02-17.

[32] Sharma, Amol; Delaney, Kevin J. (August 2, 2007). "Google Pushes Tailored Phones To Win Lucrative Ad Market" (http://online.wsj.com/article_email/SB118602176520985718-lMyQjAxMDE3ODA2MjAwMjIxWj.html). *The Wall Street Journal*. . Retrieved 2012-02-17.

[33] "Google admits to mobile phone plan" (http://web.archive.org/web/20070703031543/http://www.directtraffic.org/OnlineNews/Google_admits_to_mobile_phone_plan_18094880.html). *directtraffic.org*. Google News. March 20, 2007. Archived from the original (http://www.directtraffic.org/OnlineNews/Google_admits_to_mobile_phone_plan_18094880.html) on 2007-07-03. . Retrieved 2012-02-17.

[34] McKay, Martha (December 21, 2006). "Can iPhone become your phone?; Linksys introduces versatile line for cordless service" (http://record-bergen.vlex.com/vid/iphone-phone-linksys-versatile-cordless-62885923). *The Record (Bergen County)*: p. L9. . Retrieved 2012-02-21. "And don't hold your breath, but the same cell phone-obsessed tech watchers say it won't be long before Google jumps headfirst into the phone biz. Phone, anyone?"

[35] Claburn, Thomas (September 19, 2007). "Google's Secret Patent Portfolio Predicts gPhone" (http://www.informationweek.com/news/showArticle.jhtml?articleID=201807587&cid=nl_IWK_daily). *InformationWeek*. . Retrieved 2012-02-17.

[36] Pearce, James Quintana (September 20, 2007). "Google's Strong Mobile-Related Patent Portfolio" (http://www.moconews.net/entry/419-googles-strong-mobile-related-patent-portfolio). *mocoNews.net*. . Retrieved 2012-02-17.

[37] Martinez, Jennifer (December 10, 2008). "Corrected: Update 2: More mobile phone makers back Google's Android" (http://www.reuters.com/article/2008/12/10/openhandset-idUSN0928595620081210). *Reuters* (Thomson Reuters). . Retrieved 2012-02-16.

[38] Kharif, Olga (December 9, 2008). "Google's Android Gains More Powerful Followers" (http://www.businessweek.com/the_thread/techbeat/archives/2008/12/googles_android_2.html). *BusinessWeek*. McGraw-Hill. . Retrieved 2012-02-16.

[39] http://source.android.com/

[40] "About the Android Open Source Project | Android Open Source" (http://source.android.com/about/index.html). Source.android.com. . Retrieved 2012-02-20.

[41] "Philosophy and Goals | Android Open Source" (http://source.android.com/about/philosophy.html). Source.android.com. . Retrieved 2012-02-20.

[42] "Frequently Asked Questions | Android Open Source" (http://source.android.com/faqs.html#compatibility). Source.android.com. . Retrieved 2012-02-20.

[43] John D. Sutter (February 4, 2011). "Why does Google name its Android products after desserts?" (http://articles.cnn.com/2011-02-04/tech/google.honeycomb.android.names_1_google-android-android-os-randall-sarafa?_s=PM:TECH). *CNNTech*. . Retrieved 2012-02-15.

[44] "Android 2.3 Platform Highlights" (http://developer.android.com/sdk/android-2.3-highlights.html). *Android Developers*. 6 December 2010. . Retrieved 2012-02-20.

[45] Mithun Chandrasekhar (February 2, 2011). "Google's Android Event Analysis" (http://www.anandtech.com/show/4150/googles-android-event-analysis/2). *AnandTech*. . Retrieved 2012-02-15. "I confirmed this with Google; Honeycomb, at least in the current form, will not be coming to non-tablet devices."

[46] Rapheal, JR (January 10, 2011). "Will Android Honeycomb come to smartphones?" (http://blogs.computerworld.com/17642/android_honeycomb_smartphones). *Computerworld*. . Retrieved 2012-02-15.

[47] "Android 3.0 Platform Highlights" (http://developer.android.com/sdk/android-3.0-highlights.html). *Google*. . Retrieved 2012-02-15.

[48] "Notes on the implementation of encryption in Android 3.0" (http://source.android.com/tech/encryption/android_crypto_implementation.html). *Android.com*. . Retrieved 2012-02-15. "If you want to enable encryption on your device based on Android 3.0 aka Honeycomb"

[49] "Encrypt the phone's internal storage" (http://android.stackexchange.com/questions/4567/encrypt-the-phones-internal-storage). *Android Enthusiasts - Stack Exchange*. 8 May 2011. . Retrieved 2012-02-15. "Android 3 (Honeycomb) offers full system encryption natively."

[50] Nilay Patel (January 26, 2011). "Motorola Atrix 4G and Xoom tablet launching at the end of February, Droid Bionic and LTE Xoom in Q2" (http://www.engadget.com/2011/01/26/motorola-atrix-4g-and-xoom-tablet-launching-at-the-end-of-februa/). *Engadget*. . Retrieved

2012-02-15.

[51] German, Kent (October 18, 2011). "Ice Cream Sandwich adds tons of new features" (http://reviews.cnet.com/8301-19736_7-20122331-251/ice-cream-sandwich-adds-tons-of-new-features/?tag=mncol;txt). Reviews.cnet.com. . Retrieved 2012-02-20.

[52] Donald Melenson (May 10, 2011). "Google announces Android 3.1, available on Verizon Xoom today" (http://www.engadget.com/2011/05/10/google-announces-android-3-1/). *Engadget*. . Retrieved 2012-02-15.

[53] Crothers, Brooke (July 17, 2011). "Android 3.2 official, coming to a tablet near you" (http://news.cnet.com/8301-13924_3-20080221-64/android-3.2-official-coming-to-a-tablet-near-you/). News.cnet.com. . Retrieved 2012-02-20.

[54] Darren Murph (June 20, 2011). "Huawei MediaPad revealed first 3.2 tablet" (http://www.engadget.com/2011/06/20/huawei-mediapad-revealed-worlds-first-7-inch-android-3-2-table/). *Engadget*. . Retrieved 2012-02-20.

[55] Brad Molen (October 18, 2011). "Android 4.0 Ice Cream Sandwich now official, includes revamped design, enhancements galore" (http://www.engadget.com/2011/10/18/android-4-0-ice-cream-sandwich-now-official/). *Engadget*. . Retrieved 2012-02-15.

[56] Tim Bray (November 24, 2010). "What Android Is" (http://www.tbray.org/ongoing/When/201x/2010/11/14/What-Android-Is). *ongoing by Tim Bray*. . Retrieved 2012-02-15.

[57] "Android-x86 - Porting Android to x86" (http://www.android-x86.org/). . Retrieved 2012-02-15.

[58] *Androidology – Part 1 of 3 – Architecture Overview* (http://www.youtube.com/watch?v=QBGfUs9mQYY) (Video). YouTube. 2008-09-06. . Retrieved 2007-11-07.

[59] Paul, Ryan (February 23, 2009). "Dream(sheep++): A developer's introduction to Google Android" (http://arstechnica.com/open-source/reviews/2009/02/an-introduction-to-google-android-for-developers.ars). *Ars Technica*. . Retrieved 2012-02-15.

[60] David Meyer (February 3, 2010). "Linux developer explains Android kernel code removal" (http://www.zdnet.com/news/linux-developer-explains-android-kernel-code-removal/389733). ZDNet. . Retrieved 2012-02-20.

[61] Greg Kroah-Hartman (2010-02-02). "Android and the Linux kernel community" (http://www.kroah.com/log/linux/android-kernel-problems.html). . Retrieved 2012-02-20. *"Google shows no sign of working to get their code upstream anymore. Some companies are trying to strip the Android-specific interfaces from their codebase and push that upstream, but that causes a much larger engineering effort, and is a pain that just should not be necessary."*

[62] Brian Proffitt (August 10, 2010). "Garrett's LinuxCon Talk Emphasizes Lessons Learned from Android/Kernel Saga" (https://www.linux.com/news/embedded-mobile/mobile-linux/344486-garretta-linuxcon-talk-emphasizes-lessons-learned-from-androidkernel-saga). Linux.com. . Retrieved 2012-02-21.

[63] Brian Proffitt (April 15, 2010). "DiBona: Google will hire two Android coders to work with kernel.org" (http://www.zdnet.com/blog/open-source/dibona-google-will-hire-two-android-coders-to-work-with-kernelorg/6274). *www.zdnet.com*. . Retrieved 2012-02-20.

[64] Steven J. Vaughan-Nichols (September 7, 2010). "Android/Linux kernel fight continues" (http://blogs.computerworld.com/16900/android_linux_kernel_fight_continues). Computerworld. . Retrieved 2012-02-20.

[65] Rafael J. Wysocki (November 24, 2010). "An alternative to suspend blockers" (http://lwn.net/Articles/416690/). *lwn.net*. . Retrieved 2012-02-15.

[66] Rafael J. Wysocki (November 12, 2010). "Technical Background of the Android Suspend Blockers Controversy" (http://lwn.net/images/pdf/suspend_blockers.pdf). . Retrieved 2012-02-15. "...the most controversial parts of the Android's opportunistic suspend infrastructure are not really necessary and therefore they should not be included into the mainline kernel.... it should be possible to convert the vast majority of the Android device drivers using wakelocks to the mainline kernel code base."

[67] Steven J. Vaughan-Nichols (August 18, 2011). "Linus Torvalds on Android, the Linux fork" (http://www.zdnet.com/blog/open-source/linus-torvalds-on-android-the-linux-fork/9426). *zdnet.com*. . Retrieved 2012-02-15.

[68] Chris von Eitzen (December 23, 2011). "Android drivers to be included in Linux 3.3 kernel" (http://www.h-online.com/open/news/item/Android-drivers-to-be-included-in-Linux-3-3-kernel-1400996.html). *h-online.com*. . Retrieved 2012-02-15.

[69] Swapnil Bhartiya (January 2, 2012). "Linux 3.3 Will Let You Boot Into Android: Greg-KH" (http://www.muktware.com/news/3273/linux-33-will-let-you-boot-android-greg-kh). *muktware.com*. . Retrieved 2012-02-15.

[70] "What is Android?" (http://developer.android.com/guide/basics/what-is-android.html). *Android Developers*. July 21, 2009. . Retrieved 2012-02-15.

[71] Topolsky, Joshua (November 12, 2007). "Google's Android OS early look SDK now available" (http://www.engadget.com/2007/11/12/googles-android-os-early-look-sdk-now-available/). *Engadget*. . Retrieved 2012-02-17.

[72] "Android Supported Media Formats" (http://developer.android.com/guide/appendix/media-formats.html). *Android Developers*. . Retrieved 2012-02-17.

[73] "Flash Player 10.1 for Android 2.2 Release Notes" (http://kb2.adobe.com/cps/860/cpsid_86018.html). *Adobe Knowledgebase*. . Retrieved 2012-02-16.

[74] "RealNetworks Gives Handset and Tablet OEMs Ability to Deliver HTTP Live Content to Android Users" (http://www.realnetworks.com/press/releases/2010/RealPlayer-for-Mobile-Delivers-HTTP-Live-Content-to-Android.aspx). *realnetworks.com*. September 10, 2010. Retrieved 2012-02-16.

[75] Musil, Steven (February 11, 2009). "Report: Apple nixed Android's multitouch" (http://news.cnet.com/8301-13579_3-10161312-37.html). *CNET News*. . Retrieved 2012-02-16.

[76] Ziegler, Chris (February 2, 2010). "Nexus One gets a software update, enables multitouch" (http://www.engadget.com/2010/02/02/nexus-one-gets-a-software-update-enables-multitouch/). *Engadget*. . Retrieved 2012-02-16.

[77] "Android 3.1 Platform Highlights" (http://developer.android.com/sdk/android-3.1-highlights.html#UserFeatures). *Android Developers*. . Retrieved 2012-02-16.

[78] Bray, Tim (April 28, 2010). "Multitasking the Android Way" (http://android-developers.blogspot.com/2010/04/multitasking-android-way.html). *Android Developers*. . Retrieved 2012-02-16.

[79] "Speech Input for Google Search" (http://developer.android.com/resources/articles/speech-input.html). *Android Developers*. . Retrieved 2012-02-16.

[80] "Voice Actions for Android" (http://www.google.com/mobile/voice-actions/). *google.com*. . Retrieved 2012-02-16.

[81] JR Raphael (May 6, 2010). "Use Your Android Phone as a Wireless Modem" (http://www.pcworld.com/article/190265/use_your_android_phone_as_a_wireless_modem.html). PCWorld. . Retrieved 2012-02-16.

[82] Nancy Gohring (October 19, 2011). "Samsung, Google Unveil Latest Android OS, Phone" (http://www.pcworld.com/article/242128/samsung_google_unveil_latest_android_os_phone.html). PCWorld. . Retrieved 2012-02-16.

[83] "Sharp ISO1 Android Smartbook Headed To Japan" (http://phandroid.com/2010/03/30/sharp-iso1-android-smartbook-headed-to-japan/). Phandroid.com. 2010-03-30. . Retrieved 2012-01-01.

[84] Laura June (September 6, 2010). "Toshiba AC100 Android smartbook hits the United Kingdom" (http://www.engadget.com/2010/09/06/toshiba-ac100-android-smartbook-hits-the-united-kingdom/). *Engadget*. . Retrieved 2012-02-20.

[85] Jolie O'Dell (May 12, 2011). "Androids Unite: How Ice Cream Sandwich Will End the OS Schism" (http://mashable.com/2011/05/12/ice-cream-sandwich/). *Mashable*. . Retrieved 2012-02-20.

[86] Hollister, Sean (January 10, 2012). "Sony Smart Watch (aka Sony Ericsson LiveView 2) hands-on" (http://www.theverge.com/2012/1/10/2695959/sony-smart-watch-aka-sony-ericsson-liveview-2-hands-on). The Verge. . Retrieved 2012-02-16.

[87] Rik Myslewski (January 12, 2011). "Android-powered touchscreen Wi-Fi headphones" (http://www.theregister.co.uk/2011/01/12/now_audio_admiral_touch/). theregister.co.uk. . Retrieved 2012-01-16.

[88] "Car Player Android-Car Player Android Manufacturers, Suppliers and Exporters on" (http://www.alibaba.com/showroom/car-player-android.html). Alibaba.com. . Retrieved 2012-02-20.

[89] "Altek Leo, the 14 megapixel Android cameraphone, headed for Europe in 2011" (http://www.engadget.com/2010/10/03/altek-leo-the-14-megapixel-android-cameraphone-headed-for-euro/). Engadget. 2010-10-03. . Retrieved 2012-01-04.

[90] Will G. (December 1, 2011). "Top Android MP3 Players for 2011" (http://www.androidauthority.com/top-android-mp3-players-for-2011-36523/). Androidauthority.com. . Retrieved 2012-02-16.

[91] "Archos Smart Home Phone now available - get Android on your landline" (http://www.androidcentral.com/archos-smart-home-phone-now-available-get-android-your-landline). Android Central. 2012-01-19. . Retrieved 2012-01-30.

[92] "T-Mobile Unveils the T-Mobile G1 - the First Phone Powered by Android" (http://web.archive.org/web/20110712230204/http://www.htc.com/www/press.aspx?id=66338&lang=1033). HTC. September 23, 2008. Archived from the original (http://www.htc.com/www/press.aspx?id=66338&lang=1033) on 2011-07-12. . Retrieved 2012-02-17. AT&T's first device to run the Android OS was the Motorola Backflip.

[93] Richard Wray (March 14, 2010). "Google forced to delay British launch of Nexus phone" (http://www.guardian.co.uk/technology/2010/mar/14/google-mobile-phone-launch-delay). London: guardian.co.uk. . Retrieved 2012-02-17.

[94] David Wang (May 19, 2010). "How to Install Android on Your iPhone" (http://www.pcworld.com/article/196595/how_to_install_android_on_your_iphone.html). pcworld.com. . Retrieved 2012-02-20.

[95] "iDroid Project Wiki" (http://www.idroidproject.org/). Idroidproject.org. . Retrieved 2012-02-20.

[96] Graziano, Dan (December 28, 2011). "Pentagon approves Android device for Department of Defense, Apple still awaits clearance" (http://www.bgr.com/2011/12/28/pentagon-approves-android-device-for-department-of-defense-apple-still-awaits-clearance/). Bgr.com. . Retrieved 2012-02-16.

[97] Ravi Mandalia (December 26, 2011). "Pentagon OKs Android for DoD Usage" (http://www.itproportal.com/2011/12/26/pentagon-oks-android-dod-usage/). ITProPortal.com. . Retrieved 2012-02-16.

[98] Chris Carroll (December 9, 2011). "Android to be Approved for DoD Use Within Weeks" (http://www.military.com/news/article/2011/android-to-be-approved-for-dod-use-within-weeks.html). Military.com. . Retrieved 2012-02-16.

[99] Alexia Tsotsis (July 14, 2011). "Google Android now on 130M total devices, with 6B app downloads" (http://techcrunch.com/2011/07/14/google-android-now-on-130-million-total-devices/). TechCrunch. . Retrieved 2012-02-21.

[100] "Android Compatibility" (http://source.android.com/compatibility/index.html). *Android Open Source Project*. . Retrieved 2012-02-20.

[101] "Android Compatibility" (http://developer.android.com/guide/practices/compatibility.html). *Android Developers*. . Retrieved 2012-02-20.

[102] "Voice Actions for Android" (http://www.google.com/mobile/voice-actions/index.html). Google.com. . Retrieved 2012-02-20.

[103] Ganapati, Priya (June 11, 2010). "Independent App Stores Take On Google's Android Market" (http://www.wired.com/gadgetlab/2010/06/independent-app-stores-take-on-googles-android-market/). Wired News. . Retrieved 2012-02-20.

[104] "Android Security Overview" (http://source.android.com/tech/security/index.html). *Android Open Source Project*. . Retrieved 2012-02-20.

[105] Felt, Adrienne Porte; Chin, Erika; Hanna, Steve; Song, Dawn; Wagner, David. *Android Permissions Demystified* (http://www.cs.berkeley.edu/~afelt/android_permissions.pdf). . Retrieved 2012-02-20.

[106] Jeon, Jinseong; Micinski, Kristopher K.; Vaughan, Jeffrey A.; Reddy, Nikhilesh; Zhu, Yixin; Foster, Jeffrey S.; Millstein, Todd. *Dr. Android and Mr. Hide: Fine-grained security policies on unmodified Android* (http://www.cs.umd.edu/~jfoster/papers/acplib.pdf). .

Retrieved 2012-02-20.

[107] "First SMS Trojan detected for smartphones running Android" (http://www.kaspersky.com/news?id=207576158). Kaspersky Lab. . Retrieved 2012-02-20.

[108] Aaron Gingrich (March 6, 2011). "The Mother Of All Android Malware Has Arrived" (http://www.androidpolice.com/2011/03/01/the-mother-of-all-android-malware-has-arrived-stolen-apps-released-to-the-market-that-root-your-phone-steal-your-data-and-open-backdoor/). *Android Police*. . Retrieved 2012-02-16.

[109] Perez, Sarah (February 12, 2009). "Android Vulnerability So Dangerous, Owners Warned Not to Use Phone's Web Browser" (http://www.readwriteweb.com/archives/android_vulnerability_so_dangerous_shouldnt_use_web_browser.php). Readwriteweb.com. . Retrieved 2012-02-16.

[110] Jason Kincaid (March 5, 2011). "Google Responds To Android Malware, Will Fix Infected Devices And 'Remote Kill' Malicious Apps" (http://techcrunch.com/2011/03/05/android-malware-rootkit-google-response/). *Tech Crunch*. . Retrieved 2012-02-16.

[111] Hiroshi Lockheimer (February 2, 2012). "Android and Security" (http://googlemobile.blogspot.com/2012/02/android-and-security.html). *Official Google Mobile Blog*. . Retrieved 2012-02-16.

[112] "Antivirus for Android Smartphones" (http://www.avg.com/us-en/antivirus-for-android). AVG. . Retrieved 2012-02-16.

[113] "Mobile Security" (http://www.avast.com/free-mobile-security). Avast.com. . Retrieved 2012-02-16.

[114] "Mobile Security - System requirements" (http://www.f-secure.com/en/web/home_global/protection/mobile-security/system-requirements). F-Secure. . Retrieved 2012-02-16.

[115] "Kaspersky Mobile Security" (http://www.kaspersky.com/mobile_downloads). Kaspersky.com. . Retrieved 2012-02-16.

[116] "McAfee Mobile Security for Android" (https://www.mcafeemobilesecurity.com/products/android.aspx). Mcafeemobilesecurity.com. . Retrieved 2012-02-16.

[117] "Mobile Internet Security" (http://us.norton.com/mobile-security/). Us.norton.com. . Retrieved 2012-02-16.

[118] Steve Lohr (May 8, 2011). "Suit Opens a Window Into Google" (http://www.nytimes.com/2011/05/09/technology/09google.html?scp=1&sq=Skyhook Wireless v.Google Case Yields E Mail Insight&st=cse). *The New York Times* (NYTC). ISSN 0362-4331. . Retrieved 2012-02-16.

[119] "AppAnalysis.org: Real Time Privacy Monitoring on Smartphones" (http://appanalysis.org/faq.html). . Retrieved 2012-02-21.

[120] Ganapati, Priya (2010-09-30). "Study Shows Some Android Apps Leak User Data Without Clear Notifications | Gadget Lab" (http://www.wired.com/gadgetlab/2010/09/data-collection-android/). Wired.com. . Retrieved 2012-01-30.

[121] Woyke, Elizabeth (September 26, 2008). "Android's Very Own Font" (http://www.forbes.com/2008/09/25/font-android-g1-tech-wire-cx_ew_0926font.html). *Forbes*. . Retrieved 2012-02-16.

[122] "Brand Guidelines" (http://www.android.com/branding.html). *Android*. . Retrieved 2012-02-16.

[123] Prince McLean (August 21, 2009). "Canalys: iPhone outsold all Windows Mobile phones in Q2 2009" (http://www.appleinsider.com/articles/09/08/21/canalys_iphone_outsold_all_windows_mobile_phones_in_q2_2009.html). *AppleInsider*. . Retrieved 2012-02-16.

[124] "Gartner Says Sales of Mobile Devices Grew 5.6 Percent in Third Quarter of 2011; Smartphone Sales Increased 42 Percent" (http://www.gartner.com/it/page.jsp?id=1848514). November 15, 2011. . Retrieved 2012-02-16.

[125] "comScore Reports February 2010 U.S. Mobile Subscriber Market Share" (http://web.archive.org/web/20100503102146/http://www.mycomscore.net/Press_Events/Press_Releases/2010/4/comScore_Reports_February_2010_U.S._Mobile_Subscriber_Market_Share). *Comscore.com*. April 5, 2010. Archived from the original (http://www.mycomscore.net/Press_Events/Press_Releases/2010/4/comScore_Reports_February_2010_U.S._Mobile_Subscriber_Market_Share) on 2010-05-03. . Retrieved 2012-02-16. "RIM, 42.1%; Apple, 25.4%; Microsoft, 15.1%; Google (Android), 9.0%; Palm, 5.4%; others, 3.0%"

[126] "comScore Reports September 2010 U.S. Mobile Subscriber Market Share" (http://www.comscore.com/Press_Events/Press_Releases/2010/11/comScore_Reports_September_2010_U.S._Mobile_Subscriber_Market_Share). *Comscore.com*. November 3, 2010. . Retrieved 2012-02-20.

[127] "Android hits top spot in U.S. smartphone market" (http://news.cnet.com/8301-1035_3-20012627-94.html). August 4, 2010. . Retrieved 2012-02-20.

[128] Greg Sandoval (August 2, 2010). "More signs iPhone under Android attack" (http://news.cnet.com/8301-13579_3-20012418-37.html). . Retrieved 2012-02-20.

[129] "Apple iOS Platform Outreaches Android by 59 Percent in U.S. When Accounting for Mobile Phones, Tablets and Other Connected Media Devices" (http://www.comscore.com/Press_Events/Press_Releases/2011/4/Apple_iOS_Platform_Outreaches_Android_by_59_Percent_in_U.S). *comScore*. April 19, 2011. . Retrieved 2012-02-20.

[130] Dalrymple, Jim (April 28, 2011). "The truth about Android vs. iPhone market share" (http://www.loopinsight.com/2011/04/28/the-truth-about-android-vs-iphone-market-share/). . Retrieved 2012-02-16.

[131] Jeffrey Van Camp (Jun 28, 2011). "Google activates 500,000 Android devices a day, may reach 1 million in October" (http://news.yahoo.com/google-activates-500-000-android-devices-day-may-145858294.html). *Yahoo News*. . Retrieved 2012-02-16.

[132] Barra, Hugo (May 10, 2011). "Android: momentum, mobile and more at Google I/O" (http://googleblog.blogspot.com/2011/05/android-momentum-mobile-and-more-at.html). *The Official Google Blog*. . Retrieved 2012-02-16.

[133] Kumparak, Greg (July 14, 2011). "Android Now Seeing 550,000 Activations Per Day" (http://techcrunch.com/2011/07/14/android-now-seeing-550000-activations-per-day/). *Techcrunch*. . Retrieved 2012-02-16.

[134] "Android takes almost 50% share of worldwide smart phone market" (http://www.canalys.com/newsroom/android-takes-almost-50-share-worldwide-smart-phone-market). August 1, 2011. . Retrieved 2012-02-16.

[135] Erick Schonfeld (October 13, 2011). "Larry Page: Mobile Revenues At $2.5 Billion Run-Rate, 190 Million Android Devices" (http://techcrunch.com/2011/10/13/page-google-plus-40-million-mobile-2-5-billion/). *TechCrunch*. . Retrieved 2012-02-16.

[136] Lance Whitney (November 17, 2011). "Google: 200 million Android devices now active worldwide" (http://news.cnet.com/8301-1023_3-57326649-93/google-200-million-android-devices-now-active-worldwide/). *CNET News*. . Retrieved 2012-02-16.

[137] Charlie Sorrel (October 19, 2011). "Only 3.8 Million Honeycomb Tablets Sold So Far" (http://www.wired.com/gadgetlab/2011/10/only-3-8-million-honeycomb-tablets-sold-so-far/). Wired.com. . Retrieved 2012-02-16.

[138] "Android Platform Versions" (http://developer.android.com/resources/dashboard/platform-versions.html). *Android Developers*. February 1, 2012. . Retrieved 2012-02-16.

[139] "Google Keynote at AnDevCon II" (https://www.youtube.com/watch?v=gHm_4fC60). *Development Team*. November 9, 2011. . Retrieved 2012-02-15.

[140] Peter Dockrill (December 2, 2011). "Meet Androidland: Australia opens "world-first" Android store in Melbourne" (http://apcmag.com/meet-androidland-australia-opens-world-first-android-store-in-melbourne.htm). Apcmag.com. . Retrieved 2012-02-16.

[141] "Android Open Source Project Frequently Asked Questions: Compatibility" (http://source.android.com/faqs.html#compatibility). *source.android.com*. . Retrieved 2012-02-15.

[142] "Skyhook Wireless, Inc. vs Google, Inc" (http://daringfireball.net//misc/2010/09/Skyhook-Google Complaint and Jury Demand.pdf) (pdf). September 15, 2010. . Retrieved 2012-02-16. "This entirely subjective review, conducted solely by Google employees with ultimate authority to interpret the scope and meaning of the CDD as they see fit, effectively gives Google the ability to arbitrarily deem any software, feature or function 'non-compatible' with the CDD."

[143] "Skyhook Wireless, Inc. vs. Google, Inc." (http://www.socialaw.com/slip.htm?cid=20416&sid=121). *Social Law Library Research Portal*. December 2010. . Retrieved 2012-02-16.

[144] Boulton, Clint (October 21, 2008). "Google Open-Sources Android on Eve of G1 Launch" (http://www.eweek.com/c/a/Mobile-and-Wireless/Google-Open-Sources-Android-on-Eve-of-G1-Launch/). *eWeek*. . Retrieved 2012-02-17.

[145] Bort, Dave (October 21, 2008). "Android is now available as open source" (http://web.archive.org/web/20090228170042/http://source.android.com/posts/opensource). *Android Open Source Project*. Archived from the original (http://source.android.com/posts/opensource) on 2009-02-28. . Retrieved 2012-02-16.

[146] "Licenses: Android Open Source" (http://source.android.com/source/licenses.html). *Android Open Source Project*. . Retrieved 2012-02-16.

[147] Ryan Paul (November 6, 2007). "Why Google chose the Apache Software License over GPLv2 for Android" (http://arstechnica.com/old/content/2007/11/why-google-chose-the-apache-software-license-over-gplv2.ars). *Ars Technica*. . Retrieved 2012-02-16.

[148] "Frequently Asked Questions: What is involved in releasing the source code for a new Android version?" (http://source.android.com/faqs.html#what-is-involved-in-releasing-the-source-code-for-a-new-android-version). *Android Open Source Project*. . Retrieved 2012-02-16.

[149] Christopher Dawson (March 24, 2011). "Google Android 3.0 "Honeycomb": Open source no more" (http://www.zdnet.com/blog/google/google-android-30-honeycomb-open-source-no-more/2845). ZDNet. . Retrieved 2012-02-16.

[150] Bray, Tim (April 6, 2011). "Android Developers Blog: I think I'm having a Gene Amdahl moment" (http://android-developers.blogspot.com/2011/04/i-think-im-having-gene-amdahl-moment.html). Android-developers.blogspot.com. . Retrieved 2012-02-16.

[151] Jerry Hildenbrand (March 24, 2011). "Honeycomb won't be open-sourced? Say it ain't so!" (http://www.androidcentral.com/google-not-open-sourcing-honeycomb-says-bloomberg). Androidcentral.com. . Retrieved 2012-02-16.

[152] Thom Holwerda (November 14, 2011). "Android 4.0 Ice Cream Sandwich Source Code Released" (http://www.osnews.com/story/25330/Android_4_0_Ice_Cream_Sandwich_Source_Code_Released). *OSNews*. . Retrieved 2012-02-16.

[153] Niccolai, James (August 12, 2010). "Update: Oracle sues Google over Java use in Android" (http://www.computerworld.com/s/article/9180678/Update_Oracle_sues_Google_over_Java_use_in_Android). *Computerworld*. International Data Group Inc. . Retrieved 2012-02-16.

[154] http://worldwide.espacenet.com/textdoc?DB=EPODOC&IDX=US5966702

[155] http://worldwide.espacenet.com/textdoc?DB=EPODOC&IDX=US6910205

[156] "Oracle's complaint against Google for Java patent infringement" (http://www.scribd.com/doc/35811761/Oracle-s-complaint-against-Google-for-Java-patent-infringement). scribd.com. August 12, 2010. . Retrieved 2012-02-16.

[157] Singel, Ryan (October 5, 2010). "Calling Oracle Hypocritical, Google Denies Patent Infringement" (http://www.wired.com/epicenter/2010/10/google-oracle-android/). *Wired News*. Condé Nast. . Retrieved 2012-02-16.

[158] "Google Answers Oracle, Counterclaims, and Moves to Dismiss Copyright Infringement Claim" (http://groklaw.net/article.php?story=20101005114201136). *Groklaw*. Pamela Jones. October 5, 2010. . Retrieved 2012-02-16.

[159] "Google Files Sizzling Answer to Oracle's Amended Complaint and its Opposition to Motion to Dismiss; updated 2Xs" (http://groklaw.net/article.php?story=20101111149336O5). *Groklaw*. November 11, 2010. . Retrieved 2012-02-16.

[160] "Microsoft collects license fees on 50% of Android devices, tells Google to "wake up"" (http://arstechnica.com/microsoft/news/2011/10/microsoft-collects-license-fees-on-50-of-android-devices-tells-google-to-wake-up.ars). *Ars Technica*. . Retrieved 2012-02-16.

[161] Mikael Ricknäs (September 28, 2011). "Microsoft signs Android licensing deal with Samsung" (http://www.computerworld.com/s/article/9220357/Microsoft_signs_Android_licensing_deal_with_Samsung). *Computerworld*. . Retrieved 2012-02-16.

[162] Jacqui Cheng (August 3, 2011). "Google publicly accuses Apple, Microsoft, Oracle of patent bullying" (http://arstechnica.com/tech-policy/news/2011/08/google-publicly-accuses-apple-microsoft-oracle-of-patent-bullying.ars). . Retrieved 2012-02-16.

[163] Casey Johnston (August 15, 2011). "Google, needing patents, buys Motorola wireless for $12.5 billion" (http://arstechnica.com/gadgets/news/2011/08/google-to-buy-motorola-in-effort-to-defend-itself-from-patent-bullies.ars). . Retrieved 2012-02-16.

[164] Paul, Ryan (January 4, 2012). "Google buys another round of IBM patents as its Oracle trial nears" (http://arstechnica.com/gadgets/news/2012/01/google-buys-another-round-of-ibm-patents-as-oracle-trial-nears.ars). Ars Technica (http://arstechnica.com). . Retrieved 2012-02-16.

[165] Greene, Jay (January 3, 2012). "Google's acquisition of IBM patents may aid its Oracle case" (http://news.cnet.com/8301-1023_3-57351633-93/googles-acquisition-of-ibm-patents-may-aid-its-oracle-case/). News.cnet.com. . Retrieved 2012-02-16.

[166] Quick, Greg (February 15, 2012). "Motorola/Google Deal Gets OK-With a Warning" (http://www.mobilesportsreport.com/2012/02/motorolagoogle-deal-gets-ok-with-a-warning/). *Mobile Sports Report*. . Retrieved 2012-02-21.

External links

- Official website (http://http://www.android.com/)
- Android devices at Google.com (http://www.google.com/phone/)
- Google's Android apps (http://www.google.com/mobile/android/)
- Android (operating system) (http://www.dmoz.org/Computers/Systems/Handhelds/Android/) at the Open Directory Project
- Sergey Brin introduces the Android platform (https://www.youtube.com/watch?v=1FJHYqE0RDg) on YouTube
- Android: Building a Mobile Platform to Change the Industry (http://www.stanford.edu/class/ee380/Abstracts/071128.html): lecture given by Google Mobile Platforms Manager, Richard Miner at Stanford University (video archive (http://ee380.stanford.edu/cgi-bin/videologger.php?target=071128-ee380-300.asx))
- Android Internals: Fragment of a course detailing the architecture of Android and interaction of its components (http://technologeeks.com/Courses/Android-Excerpt.pdf)
- Diagram of Android internals (http://www.makelinux.net/android/internals/)

Tablet_computer

A **tablet computer**, or a **tablet**, is a mobile computer, larger than a mobile phone or personal digital assistant, integrated into a flat touch screen and primarily operated by touching the screen rather than using a physical keyboard. It often uses an onscreen virtual keyboard, a passive stylus pen, or a digital pen.[1] [2] [3]

The Apple iPad

The term may also apply to a variety of form factors that differ in position of the screen with respect to a keyboard. The standard form is called *slate*, which does not have an integrated keyboard but may be connected to one with a wireless link or a USB port. *Convertible* notebook computers have an integrated keyboard that can be hidden by a swivel joint or slide joint, exposing only the screen for touch operation. *Hybrids* have a detachable keyboard so that the touch screen can be used as a stand-alone tablet. *Booklets* include two touch screens, and can be used as a notebook by displaying a virtual keyboard in one of them.

Early examples of the *information tablet* concept originated in the 19th and 20th centuries mainly as prototypes and concept ideas; prominently, Alan Kay's Dynabook. First commercial portable electronic devices based on the concept appeared at the end of the 20th century. During the 2000s Microsoft attempted a relatively unsuccessful product line with Microsoft Tablet PC, which carved a niche market at hospitals and outdoor businesses. In 2010 Apple released the iPad based on the technology developed in parallel with their previous iPhone, and reached worldwide commercial success.

Background

History

The tablet computer and the associated special operating software is an example of pen computing technology, and thus the development of tablets has deep historical roots.

Electrical devices with data input and output on a flat information display have existed as early as 1888.[4] Throughout the 20th century many devices with these characteristics have been ideated and created whether as blueprints, prototypes or commercial products, with the Dynabook concept in 1968 being a spiritual precursor of tablets and laptops. In addition to many academic and research systems, there were several companies with commercial products in the 1980s.

During the 2000s Microsoft attempted to define with the Microsoft Tablet PC the *tablet personal computer* product concept[5] as a mobile computer for field work in business,[6] though their devices failed to achieve widespread usage mainly due to price and usability problems that made them unsuitable outside of their limited intended purpose.[7]

In April 2010 Apple Inc. released the iPad, a tablet computer with an emphasis on media consumption. The shift in purpose, together with increased usability, battery life, simplicity, lower weight and cost, and overall quality with respect to previous tablets, was perceived as defining a new class of consumer device[8] and shaped the commercial market for tablets in the following year.[9]

As a result, two distinctly different types of tablet computing devices exist as of 2011, the *Tablet PC* and the *Post-PC tablet*, whose operating systems are of different origin.

Traditional tablet PCs

A tablet personal computer (tablet PC) is a portable personal computer equipped with a touchscreen as a primary input device, and running a modified desktop OS[10] designed to be operated and owned by an individual.[11] The term was made popular as a concept presented by Microsoft in 2000[12] and 2001[13] but tablet PCs now refer to any tablet-sized personal computer regardless of the (desktop) operating system.[14]

Tablet personal computers are mainly based on the x86 IBM-PC architecture [15] and are fully functional personal computers employing a slightly modified personal computer OS (such as Windows or Ubuntu Linux) supporting their touch-screen, instead of a traditional display, mouse and keyboard. A typical tablet personal computer needs to be stylus driven, because operating the typical desktop based OS requires a high precision to select GUI widgets, such as a the close window button.

"Post-PC" tablets

Since mid-2010, new tablet computers have been introduced with mobile operating systems that forgo the Wintel paradigm,[16] have a different interface instead of the traditional desktop OS, and represent a new type of computing device.[17] These "post-PC" mobile OS tablet computer devices are normally finger driven and most frequently use capacitive touch screens with multi-touch capabilities instead of the simple resistive touchscreens of typical stylus driven systems.

The most successful of these was the Apple iPad using the iOS operating system.[18] Samsung's Galaxy Tab and others followed, continuing the now common trends towards multi-touch and other natural user interface features, as well as flash memory solid-state storage drives and "instant on" warm-boot times; in addition, standard external USB and Bluetooth keyboards can often be used. Most frequently the operating system running a tablet computer that's not based on the traditional PC architecture is based on a Unix-like OS, such as Darwin, Linux or QNX. Some have 3G mobile telephony capabilities.[19]

In forgoing the x86 precondition (a requisite of Windows compatibility), most tablet computers released since mid-2010 use a version of an ARM architecture processor for longer battery life versus battery weight, heretofore used in portable equipment such as MP3 players and cell phones. Especially with the introduction of the ARM Cortex family, this architecture is now powerful enough for tasks such as internet browsing, light production work and gaming.[20]

A significant trait of tablet computers not based on the traditional PC architecture is that the main source of 3rd party software for these devices tends to be through online distribution, rather than more traditional methods of boxed software or direct sales from software vendors. These sources, known as "app stores," provide centralized catalogues of software from both 1st and 3rd parties, and allow simple "one click" on-device software purchasing, installation, and updates.

Touch user interface

A key and common component among tablet computers is touch input. This allows the user to navigate easily and intuitively and type with a virtual keyboard on the screen. The first tablet to do this was the GRiDPad by GRiD Systems Corporation; the tablet featured both a stylus,a pen-like tool to aid with precision in a touchscreen device as well as an on screen keyboard.[21]

Samsung Galaxy Tab demonstrating multi-touch

The event processing of the operating system must respond to touches rather than clicks of a keyboard or mouse, which allows integrated hand-eye operation, a natural part of the somatosensory system. Although the device implementation differs from more traditional PCs or laptops, tablets are disrupting the current vendor sales by weakening traditional laptop PC sales in favor of the current tablet computers.[22] [23] [24] This is even more true of the "finger driven multi-touch" interface of the more recent tablet computers, which often emulate the way actual objects behave.

Handwriting recognition

Because tablet personal computers normally use a stylus, they quite often implement handwriting recognition, while other tablet computers with finger driven screens do not. Finger driven screens however are potentially better suited for inputting "variable width stroke based" characters, like Chinese/Japanese/Korean writing, due to their built in capability of "pressure sensing". However at the moment not much of this potential is already used, and as a result even on tablet computers Chinese users often use a (virtual) keyboard for input.[25]

Chinese characters like this one meaning "person" can be written by handwriting recognition (人 , Mandarin: *rén*, Korean: *in*, Japanese: *jin*, *nin*; *hito*, Cantonese: jan4). The character has two strokes, the first shown here in dark, and the second in red. The black area represents the starting position of the writing instrument.

Touchscreen hardware

Touchscreens are usually one of two forms;

- Resistive touchscreens are passive and can respond to any kind of pressure on the screen. They allow a high level of precision (which may be needed, when the touch screen tries to emulate a pointer for precision pointing, which in Tablet personal computers is common) but may require calibration to be accurate. Because of the high resolution of detection, a stylus or fingernail is often used for resistive screens. Although some possibility exist for implementing multi-touch on a resistive touch-screen, the possibilities are quite limited. As modern tablet computers tend to heavily lean on the use of multi-touch, this technology has faded out on high-end devices where it has been replaced by capacitive touchscreens.
- Capacitive touchscreens tend to be less accurate, but more responsive than resistive screens. Because they require a conductive material, such as a finger tip, for input, they are not common among (stylus using) Tablet PCs but are more prominent on the smaller scale "tablet computer" devices for ease of use, which generally do not use a stylus, and need multi-touch capabilities.

Other touch technology used in tablets include:

- Palm recognition. It prevents inadvertent palms or other contacts from disrupting the pen's input.
- Multi-touch capabilities, which can recognize multiple simultaneous finger touches, allowing for enhanced manipulation of on-screen objects.[26]

Some professional-grade Tablet PCs use pressure sensitive films that additionally allow pressure sensitivity such as those on graphics tablets.

Concurrently capacitive touch-screens, which use finger tip detection can often detect the size of the touched area, and can make some conclusions to the pressure force used, for a similar result.[27]

Other features

- Accelerometer: An accelerometer is a device that detects the physical movements of the tablet. This allows greater flexibility of use since tablets do not necessarily have a fixed direction of use. The accelerometer can also be used to detect the orientation of the tablet relative to the center of the earth, but can also detect movement of the tablet, both of which can be used as an alternative control interface for a tablet's software.
- Ambient light and proximity sensors are additional "senses", that can provide controlling input for the tablet.
- Storage drive: Large tablets use storage drives similar to laptops, while smaller ones tend to use drives similar to MP3 players or have on-board flash memory. They also often have ports for removable storage such as Secure Digital cards. Due to the nature of the use of tablets, solid-state memory is often preferable due to its better resistance to damage during movement.
- Wireless: Because tablets by design are mobile computers, wireless connections are less restrictive to motion than wired connections. Wi-Fi connectivity has become ubiquitous among tablets. Bluetooth is commonly used for connecting peripherals and communicating with local devices in place of a wired USB connection.
- 3D: Following mobile phone, there are also 3D slate tablet with dual lens at the back of the tablet and also provided with blue-red glasses.[28]
- Docking station: Some newer tablets are offering a optional docking station that has a full size qwerty keyboard and USB port, providing both portability and flexibility.

Form factors

Tablet computers come in a range of sizes, currently ranging from tablet PCs to PDAs. Tablet personal computers tend to be as large as laptops and often are the largest usable size for mobile tablet computing while the new generation of tablet computers can be (much) smaller and use a RISC (ARM or MIPS) CPU, and in size can border on PDAs.

Slate

Slate computers, which resemble writing slates, are tablet computers without a dedicated keyboard. For text input, users rely on handwriting recognition via an active digitizer, touching an on-screen keyboard using fingertips or a stylus, or using an external keyboard that can usually be attached via a wireless or USB connection.

Slate computers typically incorporate small (8.4–14.1 inches/**unknown operator: u'strong'unknown operator: u'strong'unknown operator: u'strong' unknown operator: u'strong'**) LCD screens and have been popular in vertical markets such as health care, education, hospitality, aviation (pilot documentation and maps),[29] and field work. Applications for field work often require a tablet computer that has rugged specifications that ensure long life by resisting heat, humidity, and drop/vibration damage. This added focus on mobility and/or ruggedness often leads to elimination of moving parts that could hinder these qualities.

Booklet

Booklet computers are dual-touchscreen tablet computers that fold like a book. Typical booklet computers are equipped with multi-touch screens and pen writing recognition capabilities. They are designed to be used as digital day planners, Internet surfing devices, project planners, music players, and displays for video, live TV, and e-reading.

Convertible

Convertible notebooks have a base body with an attached keyboard. They more closely resemble modern laptops, and are usually heavier and larger than slates.

Typically, the base of a convertible attaches to the display at a single joint called a swivel hinge or rotating hinge. The joint allows the screen to rotate through 180° and fold down on top of the keyboard to provide a flat writing surface. This design, although the most common, creates a physical point of weakness on the notebook.

A Lenovo X61 in slate mode

Some manufacturers have attempted to overcome these weak points. The Panasonic Toughbook 19, for example, is advertised as a more durable convertible notebook. Panasonic has announced the Toughpad, a water- and shockproof Android tablet. One model by Acer (the TravelMate C210) has a sliding design in which the screen slides up from the slate-like position and locks into place to provide the laptop mode.

Sliding screens were presented at CES 2011. The first product to use it is the Samsung Sliding PC7 Series,[30] a tablet with Intel Atom hardware and a unique sliding screen that allows the product to be used as a laptop or slate tablet when the screen is locked in place covering the whole keyboard. The concept still has to prove its reliability, but is intended to combine the virtues of tablet PCs with those of notebooks. Also presented was the upcoming Inspiron Duo from Dell, which rotates the screen horizontally when opened. Convertibles like that with hardware specs of a netbook are called netvertibles.

Hybrid

Hybrids, a term coined by users of the HP/Compaq TC1000 and TC1100 series, share the features of the slate and convertible by using a detachable keyboard that operates in a similar fashion to a convertible when attached. Hybrids are not to be confused with slate models with detachable keyboards; detachable keyboards for pure slate models do not rotate to allow the tablet to rest on it like a convertible.

System architecture

Two major computer architectures compete in the tablet market,[31] x86 and ARM architecture. x86, including x86-64, is popular on tablet PCs due to its use on laptops which can share common software and hardware and which can run a version of Windows. There are also non-PC based x86 tablets like the JooJoo. ARM gained popularity following the success of the iPad.[32] ARM is more power and cost efficient for mobile computing and is gaining popularity for smaller tablets from other manufacturers such as Samsung with the Galaxy Tab which runs on Android.

Operating systems and vendors

Tablets, like regular computers, can run a number of operating systems. These come in two classes, namely traditional desktop-based operating systems and post-PC mobile-based ("phone-like") operating systems.

For the former class popular OS's are Microsoft Windows, and a range of Linux distributions. HP is developing enterprise-level tablets under Windows and consumer-oriented tablets under webOS. In the latter class the popular variants include Apple iOS, and Google Android. Manufacturers are also testing the market for products with Windows CE, Chrome OS,[33] [34] and so forth.

Boot times for iPads are one-half the boot times for current Windows 7 netbooks, which can take over 50 seconds to display the login prompt.[35] The BIOS initialization for a PC, which has remained unchanged since the invention of the PC, can still take 25 seconds.[36]

Traditional Tablet PC operating systems

Microsoft

Following Windows for Pen Computing, Microsoft has been developing support for tablets runnings Windows under the Microsoft Tablet PC name.[37] According to a 2001 Microsoft definition[38] of the term, "Microsoft Tablet PCs" are pen-based, fully functional x86 PCs with handwriting and voice recognition functionality. Tablet PCs use the same hardware as normal laptops but add support for pen input. For specialized support for pen input, Microsoft released Windows XP Tablet PC Edition. Today there is no tablet specific version of Windows but instead support is built in to both Home and Business versions of Windows Vista and Windows 7. Tablets running Windows get the added functionality of using the touchscreen for mouse input, hand writing recognition, and gesture support. Following Tablet PC, Microsoft announced the UMPC initiative in 2006 which brought Windows tablets to a smaller, touch-centric form factor. This was relaunched in 2010 as *Slate PC*, to promote tablets running Windows 7, ahead of Apple's iPad launch.[39] [40] Slate PCs are expected to benefit from mobile hardware advances derived from the success of the netbooks.

Microsoft has since announced Windows 8 which will have features designed for touch input, while running on both PCs and ARM architecture.[41] Microsoft states multiple builds are needed, with 1 build for x86 processors and with 3 builds for ARM; ARM targets are defined for NVIDIA, Qualcomm, and TI processors.[42]

While many tablet manufacturers are moving to the ARM architecture with lighter operating systems, Microsoft has stood firm to Windows.[43] [44] [45] [46] Though Microsoft has Windows CE for ARM support it has kept its target market for the smartphone industry with Windows Mobile and the new Windows CE 6 based Windows Phone. Some manufacturers, however, still have shown prototypes of Windows CE-based tablets running a custom shell.[47] To date, the full Windows 7 does not yet support ARM architecture.[48]

Linux

One early implementation of a Linux tablet was the ProGear by FrontPath. The ProGear used a Transmeta chip and a resistive digitizer. The ProGear initially came with a version of Slackware Linux, but could later be bought with Windows 98. Because these computers are general purpose IBM PC compatible machines, they can run many different operating systems. However, the device is no longer for sale and FrontPath has ceased operations. It is important to note that many touch screen sub-notebook computers can run any of several Linux distributions with little customization

X.org now supports screen rotation and tablet input through Wacom drivers, and handwriting recognition software from both the Qt-based Qtopia and GTK+-based Internet Tablet OS provide promising free and open source systems for future development. KDE's Plasma Active is graphical environments for tablet.[49]

Open source note taking software in Linux includes applications such as Xournal (which supports PDF file annotation), Gournal (a Gnome based note taking application), and the Java-based Jarnal (which supports handwriting recognition as a built-in function). Before the advent of the aforementioned software, many users had to rely on on-screen keyboards and alternative text input methods like Dasher. There is a stand alone handwriting recognition program available, CellWriter, which requires users to write letters separately in a grid.

A number of Linux based OS projects are dedicated to tablet PCs, but many desktop distributions now have tablet-friendly interfaces allowing the full set of desktop features on the smaller devices. Since all these are open source, they are freely available and can be run or ported to devices that conform to the tablet PC design. Maemo (rebranded MeeGo in 2010), a Debian Linux based graphical user environment, was developed for the Nokia Internet Tablet devices (770, N800, N810 & N900). It is currently in generation 5, and has a vast array of applications available in both official and user supported repositories. Ubuntu since version 11.04 has used the tablet-friendly Unity UI, and many other distributions (such as Fedora) use the also tablet-friendly Gnome shell (which can also be installed in Ubuntu if preferred). Previously the Ubuntu Netbook Remix edition was one of the only linux distibutions offering a tablet interface with all the applications and features of a desktop distribution, but this has been phased out with the expansion of Unity to the desktop. A large number of distributions now have touchscreen support of some kind, even if their interfaces are not well suited to touch operation.

Canonical has hinted that Ubuntu will be availiable on tablets, as well as phones and smart televisions, by 2014.[50]

TabletKiosk currently offers a hybrid digitizer / touch device running openSUSE Linux. It is the first device with this feature to support Linux.

Intel and Nokia

Nokia entered the tablet space with the Nokia 770 running Maemo, a Debian-based Linux distribution custom-made for their Internet tablet line. The product line continued with the N900 which is the first to add phone capabilities. The user interface and application framework layer, named Hildon, was an early instance of a software platform for generic computing in a tablet device intended for internet consumption.[51] But Nokia didn't commit to it as their only platform for their future mobile devices and the project competed against other in-house platforms. The strategic advantage of a modern platform was not exploited, being displaced by the Series 60. [52]

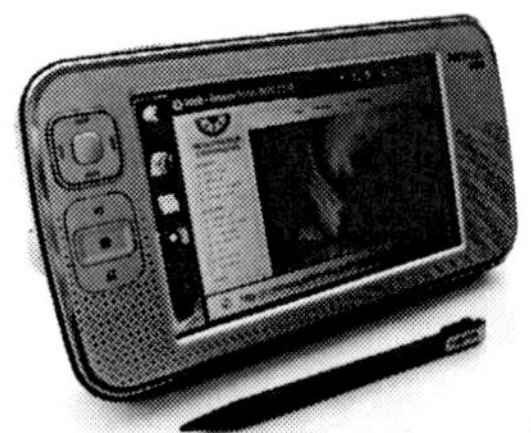

The Nokia N800

Intel, following the launch of the UMPC, started the Mobile Internet Device initiative, which took the same hardware and combined it with a Linux operating system custom-built for portable tablets. Intel co-developed the lightweight Moblin operating system following the successful launch of the Atom CPU series on netbooks. Intel is also setting tablet goals for Atom, going forward from 2010.[53] [54]

MeeGo

MeeGo is a Linux-based operating system developed by Intel and Nokia that supports Netbooks, Smartphones and Tablet PCs. In 2010, Nokia and Intel combined the Maemo and Moblin projects to form MeeGo. The first tablet using MeeGo is the Neofonie WeTab launched September 2010 in Germany. The WeTab uses an extended version of the MeeGo operating system called WeTab OS. WeTab OS adds runtimes for Android and Adobe AIR and provides a proprietary user interface optimized for the WeTab device. On 27 September 2011 it was announced by the Linux Foundation that MeeGo will be replaced in 2012 by Tizen, an open source mobile operating system.[55]

Post-PC operating systems

Tablets not following the personal computer (PC) tradition use operating systems in the style of those developed for PDAs and smartphones.

iPad

The iPad in case

The iPad runs a version of iOS which was first created for the iPhone and iPod Touch. Although built on the same underlying Unix implementation as MacOS, the operating system differs radically at the graphical user interface level. iOS is designed for finger based use and has none of the tiny features which required a stylus on earlier tablets. Apple introduced responsive multi touch gestures, like moving two fingers apart to zoom in. iOS is built for the ARM architecture, which uses less power, and so gives better battery life than the Intel devices used by Windows tablets. Previous to the iPad's launch, there were long standing rumors of an Apple tablet, though they were often about a product running Mac OS X and being in line with Apple's Macintosh computers.[56] This became partially true when a 3rd party offered customized Macbooks with pen input, known as the Modbook.

Previous to Apple's commercialization of the iPad, Axiotron introduced at Macworld in 2007[57] an aftermarket, heavily modified Apple MacBook called Modbook, a Mac OS X-based tablet personal computer. The Modbook uses Apple's Inkwell for handwriting and gesture recognition, and uses digitization hardware from Wacom. To get Mac OS X to talk to the digitizer on the integrated tablet, the Modbook is supplied with a third-party driver called TabletMagic [58]; Wacom does not provide driver support for this device.

Blackberry

The BlackBerry PlayBook is a tablet computer announced in September 2010 which runs the BlackBerry Tablet OS.[59] The OS is based on the QNX system that Research in Motion acquired in early 2010. Delivery to developers and enterprise customers is expected in October 2010. The BlackBerry PlayBook was officially released to US and Canadian consumers on April 19, 2011

Android

An ASUS Eee Pad Transformer running Android 3.2.1 Honeycomb; the keyboard is part of a docking station for the tablet.

Google's Linux-based Android operating system has been targeted by tablet manufacturers following its success on smartphones due to its open nature and support for low-cost ARM systems much like Apple's iOS. In 2010, there have been numerous announcements of such tablets.[60] However, much of Android's tablet initiative comes from manufacturers as Google primarily focuses its development on smartphones and restricts the App Market from non-phone devices.[61] Toshiba's AC100 laptop also runs on Android.[62]

There is talk of tablet support from Google coming to its web-centric Chrome OS.[63] [64]

Some vendors such as Motorola[65] and Lenovo[66] are delaying deployment of their tablet computers until after 2011, after Android is reworked to include more tablet features.[67] Android 3.0 (Honeycomb) is optimized specifically for devices with larger screen sizes, mainly tablets, and has access to the Android Market. Android is the software stack for mobile devices that includes operating system, middleware and key applications.

HP

Hewlett Packard announced the TouchPad, running webOS 3.0 on a 1.2Ghz Snapdragon CPU, would be released in June 2011. On August 18, 2011, HP announced the discontinuation of the TouchPad, due to sluggish sales.[68] HP has announced that they will release webOS as open-source.[69]

One Laptop per Child organization

The One Laptop per Child (OLPC) organization is developing a new version of the OLPC, strongly resembling a tablet computer, called the OLPC XO-3, running its "Sugar" operating system, based on Linux. The new XO-3 will be based on ARM technology from Marvell.[71]

OLPC XO-3, a tablet computer concept[70]

India

OLPC plans to introduce a tablet computer to India for $100.[72] Nicholas Negroponte, Chairman of OLPC, has invited the Indian researchers to MIT to begin sharing the OLPC design resources for their tablet computers.[73] OLPC has been awarded a grant for an interim step to their next generation tablet, OLPC XO-3.[74]

Developing software for tablet computers

The new class of devices heralded by the iPad has spurred the tendency of a walled garden approach where the vendor reserves rights as to what can be installed. The software development kits for these platforms are restricted and the vendor must approve the final application for distribution to users. These restrictions allow the hardware vendor to control the kind of software that can be used and the content that can be seen in the devices; this can be used to reduce the impact of malware on the platform and to provide material of approved content rating, and also to exclude software and content from competing vendors. The walled garden approach to application development has proven to be a competitive advantage for the iPad over HP's Touchpad, triggering HP's withdrawal from the industry, due in large part to sluggish Touchpad sales, after only 49 days on the market.[75]

Proponents of open source software deem that these restrictions on software installation and lack of administrator rights make this category one that, in their view, cannot be properly named "personal computers".[76] [77] [78] Some newer tablet computers using mobile operating systems don't use the walled garden concept, and are like personal computers in this regard.

Comparison with laptop computers

The advantages and disadvantages of tablet computers are highly subjective measures. What appeals to one user may be exactly what disappoints another. The following are commonly cited opinions of tablet computers versus laptops:

Advantages

- Usage in environments not conducive to a keyboard and mouse such as lying in bed, standing, or handling with a single hand.
- Lighter weight, lower power models can function similarly to dedicated E-book readers like the Amazon Kindle.
- Touch environment makes navigation easier than conventional use of keyboard and mouse or touch pad in certain contexts such as image manipulation, musical, or mouse oriented games.
- Digital painting and image editing are more precise and intuitive than painting or sketching with a mouse.
- The ability for easier or faster entry of diagrams, mathematical notations, and symbols.
- Allows, with the proper software, universal input, independent from different keyboard localizations.

- Some users find it more direct and pleasant to use a stylus, pen or finger to point and tap on objects, rather than use a mouse or touchpad, which are not directly connected to the pointer on screen.
- Current tablets typically have longer battery life than laptops or netbooks.

Disadvantages

- Higher price – convertible tablet computers can cost significantly more than non-tablet portable PCs although this premium has been predicted to fall.[79]
- Input speed – handwriting or typing on a virtual keyboard can be significantly slower than typing speed on a conventional keyboard, the latter of which can be as high as 50–150 WPM; however, Slideit, Swype and other technologies are offered in an effort to narrow the gap. Some devices also support external keyboards (eg: iPad can accept Bluetooth keyboards and USB keyboards through iPad Camera Connection Kit Dock Connector-to-USB adapter. Apple has also released a keyboard dock)
- Ergonomics – a tablet computer, or a folded slate PC, does not provide room for a wrist rest. In addition, the user will need to move his or her arm constantly while writing.
- More knowledge of the programs is needed – because information on e.g. icons isn't obtained by pointing at them. (The Compaq Concerto from 1992 didn't have this weakness.)
- Weaker video capabilities – Most tablet computers are equipped with embedded graphics processors instead of discrete graphics cards. In July 2010, the only tablet PC with a discrete graphics card was the HP TouchSmart tm2t, which has the ATI Mobility Radeon HD5450 as an optional extra.
- Business-oriented tablet personal computers have been slow sellers from 2001 to date.[80]
- Screen risk – Tablet computers are handled more than conventional laptops, yet many are built on similar frames; in addition, since their screens also serve as input devices, they run a higher risk of screen damage from impacts and misuse.
- Hinge risk – A convertible tablet computer's screen hinge is often required to rotate around two axes, unlike a normal laptop screen, subsequently increasing the number of possible mechanical and electrical (digitizer and video cables, embedded WiFi antennas, etc.) failure points.
- Smaller display and lack of keyboard.

Smartphone-Tablet

Since 2011 a larger screen sizes with at least 5" begun available in the market. The size is becoming very big for a smartphone and too small for a tablet, creating a hybrid category which is difficult to position. Two of them were LG Optimus Vu and Samsung Galaxy Note. Samsung claimed that they have shipped a million units of the Galaxy Note in two months.[81]

Aakash - India

The low hardware requirements and easy operation of tablet computers has made it subject to various design studies for use in developing countries, furthermore it will reduce the digital gap between the have and the have nots. Prototype tablet computers such as the Aakash have been projected to cost $35 with subsidy, according to researchers in India. It is expected to be available soon for the masses as the cheapest tablet working on Android with full functionality;[82] [83] however the bill of materials currently comes to $47 and will be available soon at retail shops at $60.[84] For the initial, the government will give them for free to students 100,000 of these tablets.[85]

See also

- Comparison of tablet computers
- Smartbook
- Ultra-Mobile PC

References

[1] http://mashable.com/follow/topics/tablets/

[2] Editors PC Magazine. "Definition of: tablet computer" (http://www.pcmag.com/encyclopedia_term/0,2542,t=tablet+computer&i=52520,00.asp). *PC Magazine*. . Retrieved April 17, 2010.

[3] Editors Dictionary.com, "tablet computer – 1 dictionary result" (http://dictionary.reference.com/browse/tablet+computer), *Dictionary.com*, , retrieved April 17, 2010

[4] Gray, Elisha (1888-07-31), *Telautograph* (http://www.freepatentsonline.com/386815.pdf), United States Patent 386,815 (full image),

[5] John Markoff, *The New York Times*, August 30, 1999, " Microsoft brings in top talent to pursue old goal: the tablet (http://www.nytimes.com/1999/08/30/business/microsoft-brings-in-top-talent-to-pursue-old-goal-the-tablet.html)"

[6] "Tablet PC: Coming to an Office Near You?" (http://itmanagement.earthweb.com/netsys/article.php/1495701/Tablet-PC-Coming-to-an-Office-Near-You.htm). .

[7] Bright, Peter Ballmer (and Microsoft) still doesn't get the iPad (http://arstechnica.com/microsoft/news/2010/07/ballmer-and-microsoft-still-doesnt-get-the-ipad.ars), Ars Technica, 2010

[8] "The iPad's victory in defining the tablet: What it means" (http://www.infoworld.com/d/mobile-technology/the-ipads-victory-in-defining-the-tablet-what-it-means-431). Infoworld. .

[9] Gilbert, Jason (August 19, 2011). "HP TouchPad Bites The Dust: Can Any Tablet Dethrone The IPad?" (http://www.huffingtonpost.com/2011/08/19/hp-touchpad-ipad-tablet_n_931593.html). *Huffington Post*. .

[10] Beck H *et al*, *Business Communication and Technologies in a Changing World*, Macmillan Education Australia, 2009, p 402

[11] Haven, Kendall F. *100 greatest science inventions of all time*, Libraries Unlimited, 2006, p 191

[12] Bill Gates introduces Tablet PC, COMDEX Nov 2000 (http://www.microsoft.com/presspass/features/2000/nov00/11-13comdex.mspx)

[13] Page, M Microsoft Tablet PC Overview (http://www.transmetazone.com/articleview.cfm?articleID=499), TransmetaZone, December 21, 2000

[14] Kuhn, Bradley M. Free software and cellphones (http://www.fsf.org/working-together/next-steps/free-software-phones), Free Software Foundation, 2010

[15] Are Intel, AMD threatened by tablet growth? Every two to three tablets sold means one lost PC sale, analyst says (http://www.marketwatch.com/story/tablet-growth-may-threaten-pc-chip-makers-2010-10-22?pagenumber=2) accessdate=2010-10-24

[16] Roger Kay on Intel and Microsoft, as quoted April 29, 2011: "Clearly, each one is looking at a post-PC world..." MarketWatch (http://www.marketwatch.com/story/microsoft-offers-more-muted-view-of-pcs-2011-04-29)

[17] Lev Grossman (Thursday, Apr. 1, 2010) " Do We Need the iPad? A TIME Review (http://www.time.com/time/business/article/0,8599,1976932,00.html)". *TIME*

[18] Worstall, Tim. *Forbes*. http://www.forbes.com/sites/timworstall/2011/07/02/ipad-one-of-the-most-successful-products-ever/.

[19] i.e. ZTE V9 Tablet and Samsung Galaxy Tab and some iPads

[20] The Coming War: ARM versus x86 (http://vanshardware.com/2010/08/mirror-the-coming-war-arm-versus-x86/) Mirror for: *The Bright Side of News* April 8, 2010

[21] Barnett, Shawn. "Jeff Hawkin" (http://www.pencomputing.com/palm/Pen33/hawkins2.html). *The man who almost single-handedly revived*. Pen Computing Magazine.

[22] Best Buy: iPad cutting into laptop sales (http://news.cnet.com/8301-13579_3-20016818-37.html)

[23] Notebook sales growth goes negative. Can we blame the iPad yet? (http://tech.fortune.cnn.com/2010/09/17/notebook-sales-growth-goes-negative-can-we-blame-the-ipad-yet/)

[24] Tablets hurt PC sales but not Macs (http://www.marketwatch.com/story/tablets-hurt-pc-sales-but-not-apples-mac-2010-10-13)

[25] China using keyboards versus tablet input (http://webcache.googleusercontent.com/search?q=cache:rX3A5F0UJKQJ:ca.news.yahoo.com/s/afp/100826/technology/lifestyle_hongkong_china_japan_culture_technology+ca.news.yahoo.com/s/afp/100826/technology/lifestyle_hongkong_china_japan_culture_technology&cd=1&hl=nl&ct=clnk&gl=nl)

[26] jkOnTheRun:So what is multi-touch? (http://jkontherun.blogs.com/jkontherun/2007/12/so-what-is-mult.html)

[27] Buxton, Bill. "Multitouch Overview" (http://www.billbuxton.com/multitouchOverview.html)

[28] T-Mobile to sell tablet with 3-D cameras, glasses http://news.yahoo.com/s/ap/20110202/ap_on_hi_te/us_tec_techbit3_d_tablet

[29] *Los Angeles Times* (September 26, 2011 (http://www.latimes.com/business/la-fi-isoldiers-20110926,0,2255882,full.story))

[30] product presentation and demo Samsung Sliding PC7 Series (http://www.alltouchtablet.com/touchscreen-tablet-news/samsung-sliding-pc-7-is-the-slider-laptoptablet-you-ever-wanted-6343/), AllTouchTablet, 2011

[31] Intel has ARM in its crosshairs (http://news.cnet.com/Intel-has-ARM-in-its-crosshairs---page-2/2100-1006_3-6210033-2.html?tag=mncol)

[32] "Apple iPad Price, Features Say "ARM" All Over" (http://www.bnet.com/blog/mobile-internet/apple-ipad-price-features-say-8220arm-8221-all-over/133). bnet. .

[33] HP vice-president Todd Bradley projects HP Slates for enterprise-level tablets, webOS for consumer-level tablets accessdate=2010-10-5 (http://www.eweekeurope.co.uk/news/hp-hints-at-business-focused-windows-7-tablet-8704)

[34] HP Slate 500 runs Win 7 Pro (http://www.csmonitor.com/Innovation/Horizons/2010/1023/HP-Slate-500-brings-professional-spin-to-the-tablet-wars), an enterprise-level tablet from HP accessdate=2010-10-23

[35] Boot time comparisons for iPad vs netbook (http://reviews.cnet.com/8301-31747_7-20001653-243.html?tag=mncol;txt)

[36] Getting a Windows PC to boot in under 10 seconds (http://news.cnet.com/8301-13924_3-20018475-64.html#ixzz12IPFj4kf)

[37] Microsoft Tablet PC (http://msdn.microsoft.com/en-us/library/ms840465.aspx)

[38] Tablet PC Brings the Simplicity of Pen and Paper to Computing: In a conversation with PressPass, Tablet PC general manager Alexandra Loeb discusses how the Tablet PC will brin... (http://www.microsoft.com/presspass/features/2000/nov00/11-13tabletpc.mspx)

[39] "Live from Steve Ballmer's CES 2010 keynote" (http://www.engadget.com/2010/01/06/live-from-steve-ballmers-ces-2010-keynote/). Engadget. . Retrieved August 4, 2010.

[40] Initial Windows 7 tablets are slated to appear during holiday 2010 season. (http://news.cnet.com/8301-13860_3-20019267-56.html?tag=mncol;mlt_related) accessdate=2010-10-19

[41] Avi Greengart of Current Analysis states "Windows 8 basically assumes that every PC is a tablet", as reported by Gordon Mah Ung et.al. (October 2011) *Maximum PC* p.27 ISSN 1522-7249

[42] Microsoft, as quoted by Mary Jo Foley, (http://www.zdnet.com/blog/microsoft/microsoft-windows-8-on-arm-to-launch-simultaneously-with-windows-8-on-intel/11875?tag=mantle_skin;content) and Microsoft blog post (http://blogs.msdn.com/b/b8/archive/2012/02/09/building-windows-for-the-arm-processor-architecture.aspx) accessdate=2012-02-09

- Gordon Mah Ung et.al. (October 2011) *Maximum PC* p.24 ISSN 1522-7249

[43] "Ballmer Admits Apple is Beating Microsoft in the Tablet Sector" (http://www.dailytech.com/Ballmer+Admits+Apple+is+Beating+Microsoft+in+the+Tablet+Sector/article19215.htm). DailyTech. . Retrieved August 6, 2010.

[44] Windows 7 is not yet optimized for fingertip events – September 24, 2010 (http://arstechnica.com/gadgets/news/2010/09/hp-slate-video-shows-all-thats-wrong-with-windows-7-on-tablets.ars)

[45] Windows 7 will not be optimized for slates; that will have to wait for Windows 8 (http://www.foxnews.com/scitech/2010/10/05/microsofts-ipad-answer-coming-christmas-holiday/)

[46] Windows 8 will not appear until 2012 (http://mashable.com/2010/10/24/microsoft-windows-8-2012/) accessdate=2010-10-24

[47] "Asus launches Eee Pad tablets and Eee Tablet note-taking thingie" (http://www.liliputing.com/2010/05/asus-launches-two-tablets-the-eee-pad-and-eee-tablet.html). liliputing. . Retrieved August 6, 2010.

[48] No Windows 7 for ARM (http://www.zdnet.com/blog/microsoft/microsoft-no-windows-7-for-arm-based-netbooks-for-now/2953?tag=mantle_skin;content) accessdate=2010-10-17

- Microsoft plans Windows tied to ARM chips (http://www.marketwatch.com/story/microsoft-plans-windows-tied-to-arm-chips-reports-2010-12-22?dist=beforebell) Dec. 22, 2010, 4:19 am EST

[49] "Plasma Active" (http://plasma-active.org/)

[50] "Ubuntu coming to tablets, phones and smart TVs by 2014" (http://www.engadget.com/2011/10/31/ubuntu-coming-to-tablets-phones-cars-and-smart-tvs-by-2014/). .

[51] Andrew Orlowski. "Nokia's Great Lost Platform" (http://www.theregister.co.uk/2011/11/21/nokia_hildon_the_great_lost_platform/) The Register

[52] "Nokia's Great Lost Platform - Page 4" (http://www.theregister.co.uk/2011/11/21/nokia_hildon_the_great_lost_platform/page4.html) .

[53] Intel shows pricing pressures for Atom due to competition from ARM (http://www.theregister.co.uk/2010/10/17/intel_tablets/) accessdate=2010-10-17

[54] Intel launches FPGA-equipped Atom (http://www.thinq.co.uk/2010/11/22/intel-launches-fpga-equipped-atom/) accessdate=2010-11-23 An FPGA, or field programmable gate array can then be custom-programmed by tablet computer vendors who have purchased these integrated circuits from the semiconductor device manufacturers

[55] Sousou, Imad. "What's Next for MeeGo" (https://www.meego.com/community/blogs/imad/2011/whats-next-meego). meego.com. . Retrieved 28 September 2011.

[56] "Apple tablet rumors redux: 10.7-inch display, iPhone OS underneath" (http://www.engadget.com/2009/09/29/apple-tablet-rumors-redux-10-7-inch-display-iphone-os-underneat/). Engadget. . Retrieved August 6, 2010.

[57] Tifanny Boggs (2007) "Axiotron and OWC Unveil the ModBook" (http://www.tabletpcreview.com/default.asp?newsID=695)

[58] http://www.thinkyhead.com/tabletmagic

[59] BlackBerry PlayBook preview (http://www.youtube.com/watch?v=eAaez_4m9mQ)

[60] "9 Upcoming Tablet Alternatives to the Apple iPad" (http://mashable.com/2010/01/27/9-upcoming-tablet-alternatives-to-the-apple-ipad/). Mashable. . Retrieved August 7, 2010.

[61] "Don't bank on KMart's $150 Augen tablet getting Android Market access" (http://www.liliputing.com/2010/08/dont-bank-on-kmarts-150-augen-tablet-getting-android-market-access.html). liliputing. . Retrieved August 7, 2010.

[62] Toshiba debuts ultraslim Android laptop (http://news.cnet.com/8301-13924_3-20008301-64.html), 21 June 2010.

[63] "Forget all these Android tablets, let me at that Chrome OS" (http://www.crunchgear.com/2010/07/20/forget-all-these-android-tablets-let-me-at-that-chrome-os/). CrunchGear. . Retrieved August 7, 2010.

[64] "Google Chrome OS Tablet Brings Ties With Verizon" (http://www.informationweek.com/news/services/data/showArticle.jhtml?articleID=226700487)

[65] Motorola Android tablet in 2011 (http://www.marketwatch.com/video/asset/digits-motorola-plans-tablet-device-2010-09-16/7CC13B36-0A8B-42E0-AD1A-72FF9BF04348)

[66] Lenovo is waiting for Honeycomb (http://www.slashgear.com/tablets-a-prescription-for-confusion-24109978/) accessdate=2010-10-24

[67] The successor to *Gingerbread*, Android project *Honeycomb* is targeted for tablet computers. – Daniel Lyons (Oct. 11, 2010), *Newsweek* p. 49

- Google demonstrated Android Honeycomb Tablet 12/7/2010 (http://www.pcmag.com/article2/0,2817,2373943,00.asp)
- Andy Rubin's demo of Motorola Honeycomb tablet (http://www.marketwatch.com/video/asset/digits-best-buys-tv-bust-2010-12-14/FD6C213F-D320-4212-BE7C-FECD5B8FEA33?dist=afterbell#!88F98ADB-3F87-49DF-AD08-385D66B0DDE8)

[68] HP Webcast announcing the end of Touchpad, webOS devices (http://www.hp.com/investor/2011q3webcast) accessdate=2011-08-18

[69] HP announces that webOS and ENYO, its application development platform, are being contributed to the open-source community. (http://www.hp.com/hpinfo/newsroom/press/2011/111209xa.html) accessdate=2011-12-09

[70] XO-3 concept design is here! | One Laptop per Child (http://blog.laptop.org/2009/12/24/xo-3-concept/)

[71] One Laptop Gets $5.6M Grant From Marvell to Develop Next Generation Tablet Computer | Xconomy (http://www.xconomy.com/boston/2010/10/04/one-laptop-gets-5-6m-grant-from-marvell-to-develop-next-generation-tablet-computer/)

[72] http://www.csmonitor.com/From-the-news-wires/2010/0723/35-computer-introduced-in-India $100 OLPC tablet computer

[73] Adam Shah (July 31, 2010), IDC, "Negroponte offers OLPC technology for $35 tablet" (http://www.goodgearguide.com.au/article/355270/negroponte_offers_olpc_technology_35_tablet/)

[74] OLPC X03 grant accessdate=2010-10-04 (http://www.xconomy.com/boston/2010/10/04/one-laptop-gets-5-6m-grant-from-marvell-to-develop-next-generation-tablet-computer/)

[75] This "vicious cycle" (slow hardware development masking slow hardware, causing slow response, causing slow software development, causing sluggish performance at an unrealistic price, causing sluggish sales) serves only to impede further software investment. "HP reboots to confront Tablet Effect" *Barron's*, August 20th, 2011

[76] Brown, Peter iPad is iBad for freedom (http://www.fsf.org/news/ibad_launch), Free Software Foundation, 2010

[77] Cherry, Steven The iPad Is Not a Computer (http://spectrum.ieee.org/consumer-electronics/portable-devices/the-ipad-is-not-a-computer), IEEE Spectrum, 2010

[78] Conlon, Tom The iPad's Closed System: Sometimes I Hate Being Right (http://www.popsci.com/gadgets/article/2010-01/ipadâs-closed-system-sometimes-i-hate-being-right), Popular Science, 2010

[79] Convertibles: The new laptop bling? – CNET News.com (http://news.com.com/Convertibles+The+new+laptop+bling/2100-1044_3-5900655.html)

[80] *PC World* (Nov 18, 2010 12:25 pm)"Why Tablet Computing Hasn't Been Big Business" (http://www.pcworld.com/businesscenter/article/211066/why_tablet_computing_hasnt_been_big_business.html)

[81] "5" Smartphones: LG Optimus Vu vs. Samsung Galaxy Note" (http://us.generation-nt.com/lg-optimus-vu-samsung-galaxy-note-smartphone-news-3384341.html). February 14, 2012. .

[82] India unveils prototype for $35 touch-screen computer (http://www.bbc.co.uk/news/world-south-asia-10740817) BBC World news-South Asia Retrieved July 25, 2010

[83] India's ($)35 PC is the future of computing (http://www.pcworld.com/businesscenter/article/201769/indias_35_pc_is_the_future_of_computing.html?tk=hp_pop) PCWorld.com

[84] Bill of materials, *Wired* (http://www.wired.com/gadgetlab/2010/07/india-35-tablet/)

[85] "India launches "world's cheapest" tablet Aakash" (http://in.reuters.com/article/2011/10/05/idINIndia-59716920111005). *Reuters*. October 5, 2011. .

External links

- Tablet or Ultrabook? (http://www.talkingabouttech.com/?p=5)
- What makes a tablet a tablet? (FAQ) (http://news.cnet.com/8301-31021_3-20006077-260.html?tag=newsLeadStoriesArea.1) CNET.com May 28, 2010

Android_Market

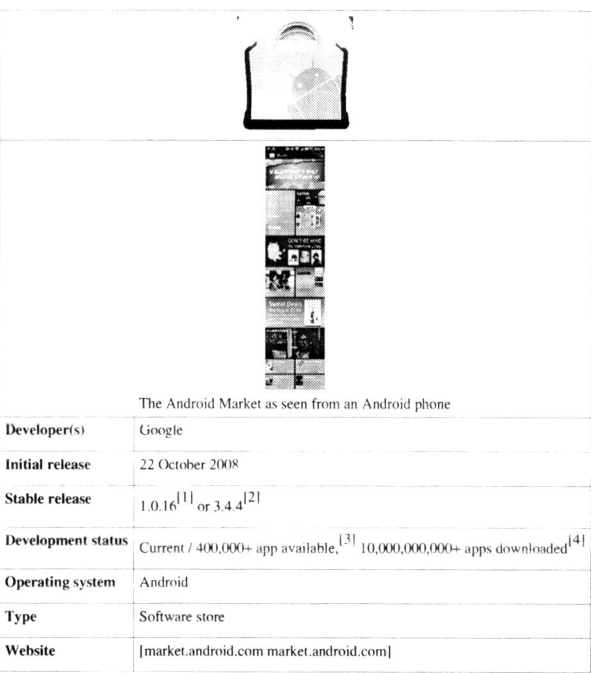

The Android Market as seen from an Android phone

Developer(s)	Google
Initial release	22 October 2008
Stable release	1.0.16[1] or 3.4.4[2]
Development status	Current / 400,000+ app available,[3] 10,000,000,000+ apps downloaded[4]
Operating system	Android
Type	Software store
Website	[market.android.com market.android.com]

Android Market is an online software store developed by Google for devices running the Android operating system. Its gateway is an application program ("app") called "Market", preinstalled on most Android devices, which allows users to browse and download mobile apps published by third-party developers. Users can also search for and read detailed information about apps on the Android Market website.

Android Market website as seen from Firefox

History

Introduction

Google announced the Android Market on August 28, 2008, and made it available to users on 22 October 2008. They introduced support for paid applications on 13 February 2009 for US and UK developers,[5] with additional support for 29 countries on 30 September 2010.[6]

Feature updates

In December 2010 Google added content filtering to Android Market and reduced the purchase refund window from 24–48 hours to 15 minutes.[7]

In February 2011 Google introduced a web client that provides access to Android Market via PC. Apps requested through the Android Market web page are downloaded and installed on a registered Android device.[8]

In May 2011 Google added new app lists to Android Market, including "Top Grossing" apps, "Top Developers", "Trending" apps, and "Editors Recommendations". Google's Eric Chu said the goal of this change was to expose users to as many apps as possible.[9]

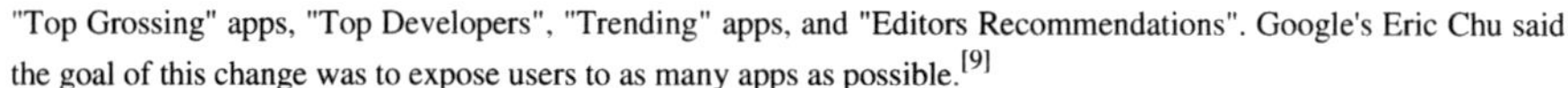

In July 2011 Google introduced a redesigned interface with a focus on featured content, more search filters, and (in the US) book sales and movie rentals.[10]

In September 2011 the Motorola Xoom tablet received an update that brought the redesigned Android Market to an Android 3.x Honeycomb based device.[11]

In November 2011 Google added a music store to the Android Market.

Applications and downloads

On 17 March 2009, about 2,300 applications were available in the Market, according to T-Mobile chief technical officer Cole Brodman.[12] On 10 May 2011, during the Google I/O, Google announced that Android Market listed 200,000 apps, and had clocked 4.5 billion apps installed.[13]

Year	Month	Applications available	Downloads to date
2009	March	2,300[12]	
	December	16,000[14]	
2010	March	50,000[15]	
	April	38,000[16]	
	August	80,000[17] [18]	1 billion
	October	100,000[19]	
2011	May	200,000[13]	3 billion[20]
	July	250,000[21]	6 billion
	October	319,000[22]	
	December	380,297[23]	10 billion[4]
2012	January	400,000[3]	

Comparisons to competitors

Android Market features 67% of free of charge apps, the highest percentage of any major app store, closely rivaled by Windows Phone Marketplace at 61%.[24] By comparison, the Apple App Store offers only 37% of their apps free of charge.[25]

App Store	Percent free of charge applications
Android Market	67%
Windows Phone Marketplace	61%[26]
Samsung Apps	39%[27]
Apple App Store	37%
BlackBerry App World	26%
Nokia Ovi Store	26%

Application use and pricing structure

Availability for users

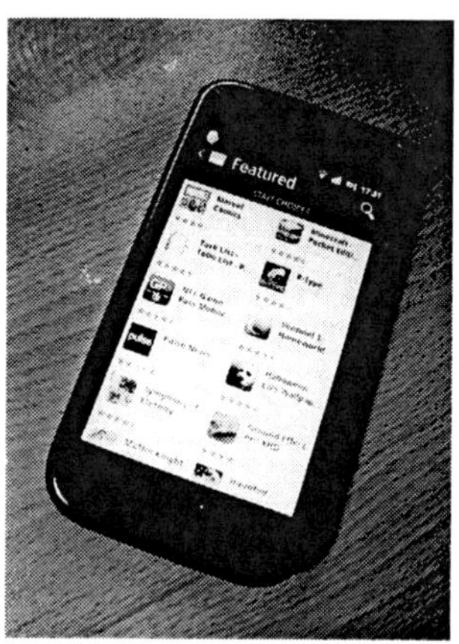

Android Market on a Samsung Galaxy S.

Android Market filters the list of applications to those compatible with the user's device. In addition, users may face further restrictions to choice of apps where developers have tied-in their applications to particular carriers or countries for business reasons. [28] Carriers can also ban certain applications, for example tethering apps.[29]

As of May 2011, users in 131 countries can purchase paid applications from Android Market.[30] Some carriers offer direct carrier billing for Android Market app purchases.[31] Purchases of unwanted applications can be refunded within 15 minutes of the time of download.[32] There is no requirement that Android applications be acquired from Android Market. Users may download Android applications from a developer's website or through a third party alternative to Android Market.

Availability for developers

The Android Market application is not open source. Only Android devices that comply with Google's compatibility requirements may install and access Google's closed-source Android Market app, subject to entering into a free-of-charge[33] licensing agreement with Google.[34] In the past, these requirements had included 3G or 4G cellular data connectivity,[35] ruling out Android-powered devices comparable to Apple's iPod touch, but this requirement had been loosened by the 2011 release of the Samsung Galaxy Player.

Developers in 29 countries may distribute applications on the Android Market.[36] However developers pay $25 for registration to distribute on the Android Market[37] . Application developers receive 70% of the application price, with the remaining 30% distributed among carriers and payment processors. Google itself does not take a percentage.[38] Revenue earned from the Android Market is paid to developers via Google Checkout merchant accounts, or via Google AdSense accounts in some countries.[39]

Approval of applications

Google places some restrictions on the types of apps that can be published, in particular not allowing "sexually explicit material", "Violence and Bullying", "Hate Speech", "Impersonation or Deceptive Behavior", copyrighted material (without permission), and a few other activities.[40] Nevertheless, developers can still distribute the apps in .apk format and they can then be installed by users on their Android devices.[41]

On 31 March 2009, Google removed all tethering applications from Android Market because they supposedly violated terms of service of certain carriers.[42] Google later restored tethering applications to Android Market, except those for the T-Mobile USA network, which was specifically the subject of the violation:[43]

> On Monday, several applications that enable tethering were removed from Android Market catalog because they were in violation of T-Mobile's terms of service in the US. Based on Android's Developer Distribution Agreement (section 7.2), we remove applications from Android Market catalog that violate the terms of service of a carrier or manufacturer.
>
> We inadvertently unpublished the applications for all carriers, and today we have corrected the problem so that all Android Market users outside the T-Mobile US network will now have access to the applications. We have notified the affected developers.

—Google, April 2009[43]

As of 20 May 2010, PDAnet, Easy Tether and Proxoid were all available in the U.S. market for T-Mobile users. On 5 April 2011, Google withdrew the Grooveshark app from Android Market due to unspecified policy violations.[44] However, the app is still available for direct download via Grooveshark's website for those users who have enabled non-market application downloads.[45] [46]

In the first quarter of 2011, at the request of the carrier, Android Market began blocking Easy Tether, and other tethering applications that do not require root access, from download to Verizon Wireless Android phones.

On 27 May 2011, Google banned SpoofApp, a Caller ID spoofing application typically used for prank calling which had been available in Android Market since 18 December 2008.[47] On 29 May 2011, Google banned the account of the developer of several video game emulators, including Nesoid, Snesoid, and N64oid and neither Google nor the developer publicly revealed the reason for the ban.[48]

Implementation details

Android Market applications are self-contained Android Package files. The Android Market does not install applications; it asks the devices's PackageManagerService to install them. The package manager is visible if the user downloads an APK file direct to their device. Applications are installed to the phone's internal storage, and under certain conditions may be installed to the devices's external storage card.[49]

Application security

Android devices can run applications written by third-party developers and distributed through Android Market and third-party application stores. Once enrolled, developers may publish their applications immediately.

Before installing an application, Android Market displays all required permissions. A game may need to enable vibration, for example, but should not need to read messages or access the phonebook. After reviewing these permissions, the user can decide whether to install the application.

Possible app permissions include functionality like:

- Accessing the Internet
- Making phone calls
- Sending SMS messages
- Reading from and writing to the installed memory card
- Accessing a user's address book data

Security software companies have been developing applications to ensure the security of Android devices. SMobile Systems, one such manufacturer, claims that 20% of apps in Android Market request permissions that could be used for malicious purposes, and 5% of apps can make phone calls without the user's intervention.[50] [51] [52] This is not a claim that the apps are actually malicious, but rather highlight the potential for malicious activity.

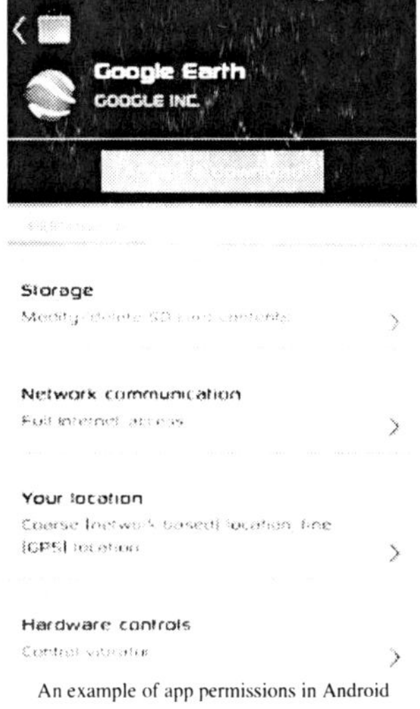

An example of app permissions in Android Market.

Security issues

In early March 2011, DroidDream, a trojan rootkit exploit, was released to the Android Market in the form of several free applications that were, in many cases, pirated versions of existing priced apps. This exploit allowed hackers to steal information such as IMEI and IMSI numbers, phone model, user ID, and service provider. The exploit also installed a backdoor that allowed the hackers to download more code to the infected device.[53] These apps were downloaded more than 50,000 times before Google took action and removed them from the Market. The exploit only affected devices running Android versions earlier than 2.3 "Gingerbread". In many cases, the only guaranteed method of removing the exploit from an infected device was to reset it to factory state, although community-developed solutions for blocking some aspects of the exploit were created.[54] Google started remotely removing the malicious apps from infected devices on March 5, and also released its own app, the "Android Market Security Tool March 2011", which automatically removed the exploit. This app was automatically installed to all infected devices, and users with infected devices were notified via e-mail.[55]

See also

- Android
- List of Android devices
- List of digital distribution platforms for mobile devices
- Android software development
- List of Android OS-related topics
- List of Open Source Android Applications
- Amazon Appstore

References

[1] https://market.android.com/details?id=com.google.android.finsky

[2] Russakovskii, Artem (14 December 2011). "Download Android Market 3.4.4 With Noticeable Speed Improvements" (http://www.androidpolice.com/2011/12/14/download-android-market-3-4-4/). *Android Police*. .

[3] "Android Market Tops 400,000 Apps" (http://www.pcworld.com/article/247247/android_market_tops_400000_apps.html). PCWorld. 04 January 2012. . Retrieved 04 January 2012.

[4] Bonnington, Christina (8 December 2011). "Google's 10 Billion Android App Downloads: By the Numbers" (http://www.wired.com/gadgetlab/2011/12/10-billion-apps-detailed/). *wired.com*. . Retrieved 12 December 2011.

[5] Chu, Eric (13 February 2009). "Android Market Update Support" (http://android-developers.blogspot.com/2009/02/android-market-update-support-for.html). .

[6] Bray, Tim (30 September 2010). "More Countries More Sellers More Buyers" (http://android-developers.blogspot.com/2010/09/more-countries-more-sellers-more-buyers.html). .

[7] "Big changes in store for Android Market" (http://www.zdnet.com/blog/burnette/big-changes-in-store-for-android-market/2151). ZDNet. 11 December 2010. . Retrieved 12 December 2010.

[8] Savov, Vlad (2 February 2011). "Android Market gets a web store with OTA installations, in-app purchases coming soon" (http://www.engadget.com/2011/02/02/android-market-gets-a-web-store/). *Engadget*. AOL Inc. .

[9] Hachman, Mark (11 May 2011). "Google Revamps Android Market to Give App Recommendations" (http://news.yahoo.com/s/zd/20110511/tc_zd/264342). *PC Magazine*. . Retrieved 17 May 2011.

[10] Montoy-Wilson, Paul (12 July 2011). "A new Android Market for phones, with books and movies - Official Google Mobile Blog" (http://googlemobile.blogspot.com/2011/07/new-android-market-for-phones-with.html). *Google Mobile blog*. . Retrieved 3 October 2011.

[11] Burns, Chris (29 September 2011). "Android Market update released for Honeycomb tablets" (http://www.slashgear.com/android-market-update-released-for-honeycomb-tablets-29184161/). *SlashGear*. . Retrieved 3 October 2011.

[12] Lawson, Stephen (17 March 2009). "Market Needs More Filters, T-Mobile Says" (http://www.pcworld.com/article/161410/android_market_needs_more_filters_tmobile_says.html). *PC World*. .

[13] Barra, Hugo (10 May 2011). "Android: momentum, mobile and more at Google I/O" (http://googleblog.blogspot.com/2011/05/android-momentum-mobile-and-more-at.html). *The Official Google Blog*. . Retrieved 10 May 2011.

[14] "Google: Actually, We Count Only 16,000 Apps In Android Market" (http://techcrunch.com/2009/12/16/google-android-market/). TechCrunch. 16 December 2009. . Retrieved 4 January 2012.

[15] Chan, Casey (18 March 2010). "Android Market has 30,000 apps, sort of" (http://www.androidcentral.com/android-market-has-30000-apps). Android Central. . Retrieved 4 January 2012.

[16] Nickinson, Phil (15 April 2010). "Android Market now has 38,000 apps" (http://www.androidcentral.com/android-market-now-has-38000-apps). Android Central. . Retrieved 4 January 2012.

[17] Hildenbrand, Jerry (9 September 2010). "Android Market has more than 80,000 apps, Android's Rubin says" (http://www.androidcentral.com/googles-andy-rubin-says-over-80k-apps-now-android-market). Android Central.

[18] "Android Market Hits 1 Billion Downloads & 100,000 apps" (http://www.fonehome.co.uk/2010/07/16/android-market-hits-1-billion-downloads-100000-apps/). 15 July 2009. . Retrieved 4 January 2012.

[19] Gibb, Kyle (26 October 2010). "Android Market passes 100,000 apps" (http://www.androidcentral.com/android-market-surpasses-100000-apps). Android Central. . Retrieved 4 January 2012.

[20] Rao, Leena (14 April 2011). "Google: 3 Billion Android Apps Installed; Downloads Up 50 Percent From Last Quarter" (http://techcrunch.com/2011/04/14/google-3-billion-android-apps-installed-up-50-percent-from-last-quarter/). *Techcrunch*. . Retrieved 13 May 2011.

[21] Nickinson, Phil (14 July 2011). "Android Market now has more than a quarter-million applications" (http://www.androidcentral.com/android-market-now-has-more-quarter-million-applications). *Android Central*. . Retrieved 14 July 2011.

[22] "Android Market reaches 500,000 app mark" (http://www.t3.com/news/android-market-reaches-500000-app-mark). www.t3.com. 2011-10-23. . Retrieved 2011-10-23.

[23] "Google Android Market" (http://www.distimo.com/appstores/app-store/19-Google_Android_Market). Distimo. 17 October 2011. . Retrieved 18 December 2011.

[24] "Windows Phone 7 Applist" (http://wp7applist.com/en-US/stats/). 20 Jan 2012. .

[25] Wehner, Mike (18 October 2011). "Google Android has double the number of free apps than Apple's App Store" (http://news.yahoo.com/blogs/technology-blog/apple-approves-500-000th-app-care-160140999.html). Yahoo. . Retrieved 18 October 2011.

[26] "Windows Phone 7 Applist" (http://wp7applist.com/en-US/stats/). 20 Jan 2012. .

[27] "Fast 12.000 Apps für Bada verfügbar" (http://allaboutsamsung.de/2011/10/fast-12-000-apps-fur-bada-verfugbar/). 31 Oct 2011. .

[28] "Android Compatibility" (http://developer.android.com/guide/practices/compatibility.html). *Android Developers*. . Retrieved 31 December 2010.

[29] O'Brien, Terrence (2 May 2011). "Carriers crack down on Android tethering apps, rain on our mobile hotspot parade" (http://www.engadget.com/2011/05/02/carriers-crack-down-on-android-tethering-apps-rain-on-our-mobil/). *Engadget*. AOL Inc. . Retrieved 15 May 2011.

[30] "Paid App Availability" (http://www.google.com/support/androidmarket/bin/answer.py?hl=en&answer=143779). Android Market Help. .

[31] Chu, Eric (13 April 2011). "Android Developers Blog: New Carrier Billing Options on Android Market" (http://android-developers.blogspot.com/2011/04/new-carrier-billing-options-on-android.html). *android-developers.blogspot.com*. . Retrieved 15 May 2011.

[32] "Returning apps" (https://support.google.com/androidmarket/bin/answer.py?hl=en&answer=134336&topic=1046718&ctx=topic). *Android Market*. Google. . Retrieved January 09, 2012. "You have **15 minutes** from the time of download to return an application purchased through Android Market for a full refund."

[33] http://source.android.com/faqs.html#how-much-does-compatibility-certification-cost

[34] "Android Compatibility" (http://source.android.com/compatibility/). *Android Open Source Project*. . Retrieved 31 December 2010.

[35] Sam Churchill. Android Tablets Need 3G/4G for Market Support (http://www.dailywireless.org/2010/09/10/android-tablets-need-3g4g-for-market-support/). dailywireless.org. 10 September 2010. Accessed 9 February 2012.

[36] "Supported locations for merchants" (http://www.google.com/support/androidmarket/bin/answer.py?hl=en&answer=150324). Android Market Help. .

[37] http://support.google.com/androidmarket/developer/bin/answer.py?hl=en&answer=113468&ctx=cb&src=cb&cbid=-8w6cs0nksvn

[38] Chu, Eric (22 October 2008). "Android Developers Blog: Android Market: Now available for users" (http://android-developers.blogspot.com/2008/10/android-market-now-available-for-users.html). *Android Developers Blog*. . Retrieved 17 May 2011.

[39] "Processing orders and receiving payouts" (https://www.google.com/support/androidmarket/developer/bin/answer.py?hl=en&answer=137997). *Android Market for Developer Help*. . Retrieved 17 May 2011.

[40] "Android.com" (http://www.android.com/us/developer-content-policy.html). Android.com. . Retrieved 2012-01-05.

[41] "3 ways to install applications on Android without the Market" (http://maketecheasier.com/install-applications-without-the-market/2011/01/28). Maketecheasier.com. 2011-01-28. . Retrieved 2012-01-05.

[42] "Banned from the Market... ok." (http://www.falsedichotomies.org/node/73). False Dichotomies. . Retrieved 26 May 2010.

[43] Krazit, Tom (2 April 2009). "Google restores tethering app for Android users outside U.S. | Wireless" (http://news.cnet.com/8301-1035_3-10210515-94.html). *CNET News*. CBS Interactive. . Retrieved 26 May 2010.

[44] "Google boots Grooveshark from Android Market" (http://news.cnet.com/8301-31001_3-20051156-261.html). *CNET*. CBS Interactive. 6 April 2011. . Retrieved 26 April 2011.

[45] "Grooveshark Mobile Music: Android" (http://mobile.grooveshark.com/phones/android). Grooveshark. . Retrieved 26 April 2011.

[46] Kumparak, Greg (April 18, 2011). "Grooveshark Back On Android, Bypasses The Android App Market" (http://techcrunch.com/2011/04/18/grooveshark-back-on-android-skips-the-app-market/). *TechCrunch*. . Retrieved January 09, 2012. "Today, Grooveshark makes its triumphant return to Android, albeit not through the official App Market. Playing on Android's ability to install third-party applications through the browser, Grooveshark has taken on the responsibility of distributing the application themselves [...]"

[47] SpoofApp Banned From Android Market (http://www.spoofcard.com/blog/2011/07/11/spoofapp-banned-from-the-android-market/). Google bans SpoofApp.

[48] "Google Pulls Yongzh's Emulator Apps Off Android Market" (http://www.pcmag.com/article2/0,2817,2386126,00.asp). *PC Magazine*. 29 May 2011. . Retrieved 29 May 2011.
[49] "App Install Location | Android Developers" (http://developer.android.com/guide/appendix/install-location.html). Developer.android.com. 15 March 2011. . Retrieved 22 March 2011.
[50] "SMobile Systems Analysis of Android App Store Reveals Massive Potential for Malware and Viruses" (http://www.prnewswire.com/news-releases/smobile-systems-analysis-of-android-app-store-reveals-massive-potential-for-malware-and-viruses-96896999.html). prnewswire.com. 22 June 2009. . Retrieved 27 June 2010.
[51] Vennon, Troy; Stroop, David (22 June 2009). "Threat Analysis of the Android Market" (http://threatcenter.smobilesystems.com/wp-content/uploads/2010/06/Android-Market-Threat-Analysis-6-22-10-v1.pdf). SMobile Systems Inc. . Retrieved 27 June 2010.
[52] "20 % des applications de l'Android Market demandent l'accès à des données personnelles" (http://www.lemonde.fr/technologies/article/2010/06/23/20-des-applications-de-l-android-market-demandent-l-acces-a-des-donnees-personnelles_1377745_651865.html). *Le Monde*. France. 23 June 2009. . Retrieved 27 June 2010.
[53] "The Mother Of All Android Malware Has Arrived: Stolen Apps Released To The Market That Root Your Phone, Steal Your Data, And Open Backdoor" (http://www.androidpolice.com/2011/03/01/the-mother-of-all-android-malware-has-arrived-stolen-apps-released-to-the-market-that-root-your-phone-steal-your-data-and-open-backdoor/). Android Police. . Retrieved 22 March 2011.
[54] "Malware Monster: DroidDream Is An Android Nightmare, And We've Got More Details" (http://www.androidpolice.com/2011/03/02/update-on-the-malware-monster-droiddream-is-an-android-nightmare-and-weve-got-more-details/). Android Police. . Retrieved 22 March 2011.
[55] "An Update on Android Market Security" (http://googlemobile.blogspot.com/2011/03/update-on-android-market-security.html). Googlemobile.blogspot.com. 5 March 2011. . Retrieved 22 March 2011.

External links

- Official website (http://www.android.com/market)
- Google Applications at the Android Market (https://market.android.com/developer?pub=Google+Inc.)

Random-access_memory

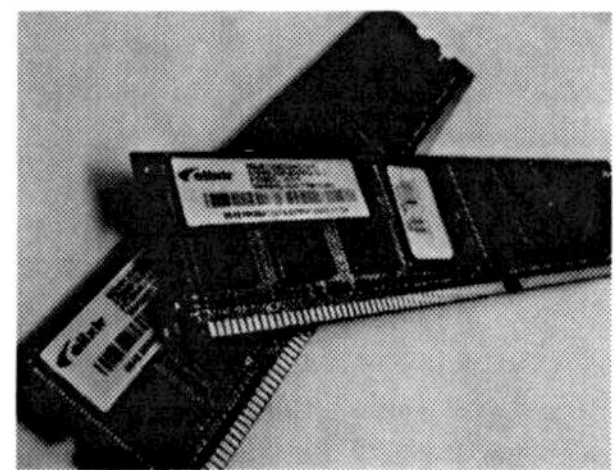

Example of writable volatile random-access memory: Synchronous Dynamic RAM modules, primarily used as main memory in personal computers, workstations, and servers.

Random access memory (**RAM**) is a form of computer data storage. Today, it takes the form of integrated circuits that allow stored data to be accessed in any order with a worst case performance of constant time. Strictly speaking, modern types of DRAM are therefore not random access, as data is read in bursts, although the name DRAM / RAM has stuck. However, many types of SRAM, ROM, OTP, and NOR flash are still random access even in a strict sense. RAM is often associated with volatile types of memory (such as DRAM memory modules), where its stored information is lost if the power is removed. Many other types of non-volatile memory are RAM as well, including most types of ROM and a type of flash memory called *NOR-Flash*. The first RAM modules to come into the market were created in 1951 and were sold until the late 1960s and early 1970s.

Other memory devices (magnetic tapes, floppy discs, CDs and DVDs) can access the storage data only in a predetermined order, because of mechanical design limitations.

History

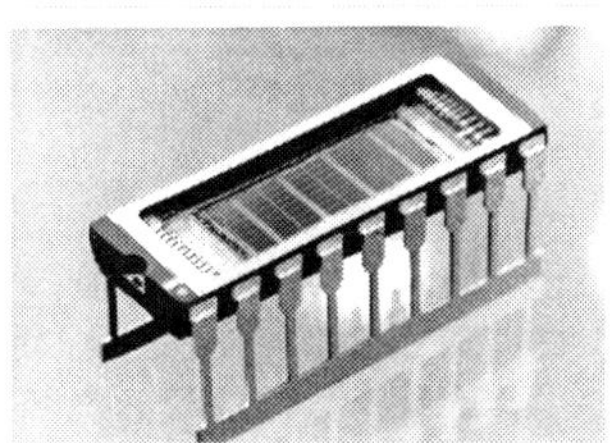

1 Megabit chip - one of the last models developed by VEB Carl Zeiss Jena in 1989

Early computers used relays, or delay lines for "main" memory functions. Ultrasonic delay lines could only reproduce data in the order it was written. Drum memory could be expanded at low cost but retrieval of non-sequential memory items required knowledge of the physical layout of the drum to optimize speed. Latches built out of vacuum tube triodes, and later, out of discrete transistors, were used for smaller and faster memories such as random-access register banks and registers. Such registers were relatively large, power-hungry and too costly to use for large amounts of data; generally only a few hundred or few thousand bits of such memory could be provided.

The first practical form of random-access memory was the Williams tube starting in 1947. It stored data as electrically-charged spots on the face of a cathode ray tube. Since the electron beam of the CRT could read and write the spots on the tube in any order, memory was random-access. The capacity of the Williams tube was a few hundred to around a thousand bits, but it was much smaller, faster, and more power-efficient than using individual vacuum tube latches.

Magnetic core memory invented in 1947 and developed up until the mid 1970's became a widespread form of random access memory. It relied on an array of magnetized rings; by changing the sense of magnetization, data could be stored, with each bit represented physically by one ring. Since every ring had a combination of address wires to select and read or write it, access to any memory location in any sequence was possible.

Magnetic core memory was the standard form of memory system until displaced by solid-state memory in integrated circuits, starting in the early 1970's. Robert H. Dennard invented Dynamic random access memory in 1968; this allowed replacement of a 4 or 6-transistor latch circuit by a single transistor for each memory bit, greatly increasing memory density at the cost of voltatility. Data was stored in the tiny capacitance of each transistor, and had to be periodically refreshed in a few milliseconds before the charge could leak away.

Prior to the development of integrated Read-only memory (ROM) circuits, *permanent* (or *read-only*) random-access memory was often constructed using diode matrices driven by address decoders, or specially wound core rope memory planes.

Types of RAM

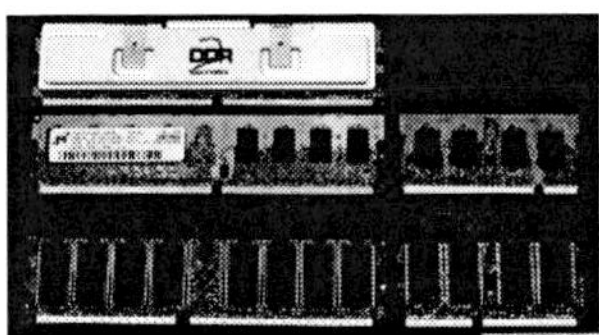

Top L-R, DDR2 with heat-spreader, DDR2 without heat-spreader, Laptop DDR2, DDR, Laptop DDR

The two main forms of modern RAM are static RAM (SRAM) and dynamic RAM (DRAM). In static RAM, a bit of data is stored using the state of a flip-flop. This form of RAM is more expensive to produce, but is generally faster and requires less power than DRAM and, in modern computers, is often used as cache memory for the CPU. DRAM stores a bit of data using a transistor and capacitor pair, which together comprise a memory cell. The capacitor holds a high or low charge (1 or 0, respectively), and the transistor acts as a switch that lets the control circuitry on the chip read the capacitor's state of charge or change it. As this form of memory is less expensive to produce than static RAM, it is the predominant form of computer memory used in modern computers.

Both static and dynamic RAM are considered *volatile*, as their state is lost or reset when power is removed from the system. By contrast, Read-only memory (ROM) stores data by permanently enabling or disabling selected transistors, such that the memory cannot be altered. Writeable variants of ROM (such as EEPROM and flash memory) share properties of both ROM and RAM, enabling data to persist without power and to be updated without requiring special equipment. These persistent forms of semiconductor ROM include USB flash drives, memory cards for cameras and portable devices, etc. As of 2007, NAND flash has begun to replace older forms of persistent storage, such as magnetic disks and tapes, while NOR flash is being used in place of ROM in netbooks and rugged computers, since it is capable of true random access, allowing direct code execution.

ECC memory (which can be either SRAM or DRAM) includes special circuitry to detect and/or correct random faults (memory errors) in the stored data, using parity bits or error correction code.

In general, the term *RAM* refers solely to solid-state memory devices (either DRAM or SRAM), and more specifically the main memory in most computers. In optical storage, the term DVD-RAM is somewhat of a misnomer since, like CD-RW, a rewriteable DVD must be erased before it can be rewritten.

Memory hierarchy

One can read and over-write data in RAM. Many computer systems have a memory hierarchy consisting of CPU registers, on-die SRAM caches, external caches, DRAM, paging systems, and virtual memory or swap space on a hard drive. This entire pool of memory may be referred to as "RAM" by many developers, even though the various subsystems can have very different access times, violating the original concept behind the *random access* term in RAM. Even within a hierarchy level such as DRAM, the specific row, column, bank, rank, channel, or interleave organization of the components make the access time variable, although not to the extent that rotating storage media or a tape is variable. The overall goal of using a memory hierarchy is to obtain the higher possible average access performance while minimizing the total cost of the entire memory system (generally, the memory hierarchy follows the access time with the fast CPU registers at the top and the slow hard drive at the bottom).

In many modern personal computers, the RAM comes in an easily upgraded form of modules called memory modules or DRAM modules about the size of a few sticks of chewing gum. These can quickly be replaced should they become damaged or when changing needs demand more storage capacity. As suggested above, smaller amounts of RAM (mostly SRAM) are also integrated in the CPU and other ICs on the motherboard, as well as in hard-drives, CD-ROMs, and several other parts of the computer system.

Other uses of RAM

In addition to serving as temporary storage and working space for the operating system and its applications, RAM is used in numerous other ways.

Virtual memory

Most modern operating systems employ a method of extending RAM capacity, known as "virtual memory". A portion of the computer's hard drive is set aside for a *paging file* or a *scratch partition*, and the combination of physical RAM and the paging file form the system's total memory. (For example, if a computer has 2 GB of RAM and a 1 GB page file, the operating system has 3 GB total memory available to it.) When the system runs low on physical memory, it can "swap" portions of RAM to the paging file to make room for new data, as well as to read previously swapped information back into RAM. Excessive use of this mechanism results in thrashing and generally hampers overall system performance, mainly because hard drives are far slower than RAM.

RAM disk

Software can "partition" a portion of a computer's RAM, allowing it to act as a much faster hard drive that is called a RAM disk. A RAM disk loses the stored data when the computer is shut down, unless memory is arranged to have a standby battery source.

Shadow RAM

Sometimes, the contents of a relatively slow ROM chip are copied to read/write memory to allow for shorter access times. The ROM chip is then disabled while the initialized memory locations are switched in on the same block of addresses (often write-protected). This process, sometimes called *shadowing*, is fairly common in both computers and embedded systems.

As a common example, the BIOS in typical personal computers often has an option called "use shadow BIOS" or similar. When enabled, functions relying on data from the BIOS's ROM will instead use DRAM locations (most can also toggle shadowing of video card ROM or other ROM sections). Depending on the system, this may not result in increased performance, and may cause incompatibilities. For example, some hardware may be inaccessible to the operating system if shadow RAM is used. On some systems the benefit may be hypothetical because the BIOS is not used after booting in favor of direct hardware access. Free memory is reduced by the size of the shadowed ROMs.[1]

Recent developments

Several new types of *non-volatile* RAM, which will preserve data while powered down, are under development. The technologies used include carbon nanotubes and approaches utilizing the magnetic tunnel effect. Amongst the 1st generation MRAM, a 128 KiB (128×2^{10} bytes) magnetic RAM (MRAM) chip was manufactured with 0.18 µm technology in the summer of 2003. In June 2004, Infineon Technologies unveiled a 16 MiB (16×2^{20} bytes) prototype again based on 0.18 µm technology. There are two 2nd generation techniques currently in development: Thermal Assisted Switching (TAS)[2] which is being developed by Crocus Technology, and Spin Torque Transfer (STT) on which Crocus, Hynix, IBM, and several other companies are working.[3] Nantero built a functioning carbon nanotube memory prototype 10 GiB (10×2^{30} bytes) array in 2004. Whether some of these technologies will be able to eventually take a significant market share from either DRAM, SRAM, or flash-memory technology, however, remains to be seen.

Since 2006, "Solid-state drives" (based on flash memory) with capacities exceeding 256 gigabytes and performance far exceeding traditional disks have become available. This development has started to blur the definition between traditional random access memory and "disks", dramatically reducing the difference in performance.

Some kinds of random-access memory, such as "EcoRAM", are specifically designed for server farms, where low power consumption is more important than speed.[4]

Memory wall

The "memory wall" is the growing disparity of speed between CPU and memory outside the CPU chip. An important reason for this disparity is the limited communication bandwidth beyond chip boundaries. From 1986 to 2000, CPU speed improved at an annual rate of 55% while memory speed only improved at 10%. Given these trends, it was expected that memory latency would become an overwhelming bottleneck in computer performance.[5]

Currently, CPU speed improvements have slowed significantly partly due to major physical barriers and partly because current CPU designs have already hit the memory wall in some sense. Intel summarized these causes in their Platform 2015 documentation (PDF) [6]

> "First of all, as chip geometries shrink and clock frequencies rise, the transistor leakage current increases, leading to excess power consumption and heat... Secondly, the advantages of higher clock speeds are in part negated by memory latency, since memory access times have not been able to keep

pace with increasing clock frequencies. Third, for certain applications, traditional serial architectures are becoming less efficient as processors get faster (due to the so-called Von Neumann bottleneck), further undercutting any gains that frequency increases might otherwise buy. In addition, partly due to limitations in the means of producing inductance within solid state devices, resistance-capacitance (RC) delays in signal transmission are growing as feature sizes shrink, imposing an additional bottleneck that frequency increases don't address."

The RC delays in signal transmission were also noted in Clock Rate versus IPC: The End of the Road for Conventional Microarchitectures [7] which projects a maximum of 12.5% average annual CPU performance improvement between 2000 and 2014. The data on Intel Processors [8] clearly shows a slowdown in performance improvements in recent processors. However, Intel's Core 2 Duo processors (codenamed Conroe) showed a significant improvement over previous Pentium 4 processors; due to a more efficient architecture, performance increased while clock rate actually decreased.

See also

- CAS latency (CL)
- Dual-channel architecture
- Triple-channel architecture
- Registered/buffered memory
- RAM parity
- Memory Interconnect/RAM buses
- Memory Geometry

Notes and references

[1] "Shadow Ram" (http://hardwarehell.com/articles/shadowram.htm). . Retrieved 2007-07-24.
[2] The Emergence of Practical MRAM http://www.crocus-technology.com/pdf/BH%20GSA%20Article.pdf
[3] http://www.eetimes.com/news/latest/showArticle.jhtml?articleID=218000269
[4] "EcoRAM held up as less power-hungry option than DRAM for server farms" (http://blogs.zdnet.com/green/?p=1165) by Heather Clancy 2008
[5] The term was coined in (http://www.eecs.ucf.edu/~lboloni/Teaching/EEL5708_2006/slides/wulf94.pdf).
[6] http://epic.hpi.uni-potsdam.de/pub/Home/TrendsAndConceptsII2010/HW_Trends_borkar_2015.pdf
[7] http://www.cs.utexas.edu/users/cart/trips/publications/isca00.pdf
[8] http://www.intel.com/pressroom/kits/quickreffam.htm

External links

- Memory Prices (1957-2010) (http://www.jcmit.com/memoryprice.htm)

DataWind

Type	Private
Industry	Computer hardware
Founded	2001 (Montreal, Canada)
Headquarters	London, United Kingdom[1]
Key people	Suneet Tuli, CEO Raja Tuli, Co-founder, CTO David Elder,COO
Products	Aakash tablet Ubislate 7 PocketSurfer Pocketsurfer2 Pocketsurfer3
Website	www.datawind.com [2]

DataWind is a British manufacturing and marketing company that produce wireless web access products, originally founded in Montreal[1] in 2001[3] by brothers Suneet and Raja Tuli[3] from the Indian state of Punjab.[4] Now headquartered in London, the company also has offices in Amritsar, Punjab, India; Dallas,Texas, US; and Mississauga, Ontario, Canada.[1]

With its research and development based in Montreal, the company until 2010 marketed its production primarily in the UK, where it is registered as an LLC.[5] In 2004, the company was described as a "small tech shop"[6] marketing its key product, the Pocketsurfer, a pda/cell phone/web browser device. Several iterations of the Pocketsurfer followed.

Datawind is now widely known for its development of the Aakash, an inexpensive tablet computer developed in conjunction with India's Minister for Human Resource Development (MHRD) and now seen as a way for the country to leapfrog the problems of educating its large population.[4] Following a development process beset by delays and setbacks,[3] the tablet will be offered at a sufficiently low price threshold – distributed by the government to students at a subsized price of $35[3] and to the public (as the *Ubislate 7*) for $60[3] – to enable ubiquitous,[3] nationwide internet use. At the subsidized price, the tablet will cost about the price of a pair of shoes[7] or a basic cell phone.[4]

Aakash tablet

In 2010 the company won an Indian government tender[3] to design the Aakash tablet computer[8] – now under manufacture by the Indian company, Quad, in an initial trial run of 100,000 units.[5] The Wall Street Journal called the Aakash, "the world's cheapest tablet."[9]

The seven-inch touch-screen tablet[1] [3] was co-developed with Datawind and Indian Institute of Technology Rajasthan[9] as part of the country's aim to link 25,000 colleges and 400 universities in an e-learning program[10] with an ultimate production goal of tens of millions of units.[5] Datawind projects the Indian government will buy 8 million to 10 million devices by early 2012.[11] Time Magazine reported in 2011 that Datawind is considering marketing tailored variants of the Aakash in the U.K., the U.S. and Latin America.[12]

In a 2011 interview, the company said it lowered the price of the tablet by developing patents to shift the device's processing burden to "backend servers in the cloud,"[13] by eliminating middle men whenever possible (DataWind itself designed the Aakash's boards, integrated components in-house and made the device's touch panel[14]), and by monetizing the operating system – that is, selling apps for the device through its own app store.[13] Despite using the Android operating system, the device does not have access to the Android Market.[7]

Future

"Not in my wildest dream I could have imagined this. Six months ago, the expectation for the tablet market was 2.5 lakh units a year. While talking to distributors, we would say we want to produce one lakh units in India, and they told us that if we were to sell 2,000 units a month, we should be happy. Now, we are looking at producing over four lakh units a month."[15]

-Datawind CEO Suneet Singh Tuli,13 Jan 2012(on huge demand of Aakash)

ITPro India and other sources reported that Datawind is co-developing the world's least expensive 4G-enabled tablet with Reliance Industries.[16]

Following the announcement of the Aakash, Datawind met Swedish Foreign Minister Carl Bildt.[17]

From being a $10-million company, Datawind is now aspiring to become a half-a-billion-dollar company in just 12 months.

See also

- List of technology companies in Montreal
- Comparison of Android devices
- Comparison of tablet computers
- OLPC
- Aakash (tablet)

References

[1] "Aakash tablet will end 'digital divide'" (http://www.montrealgazette.com/technology/Aakash+tablet+will+digital+divide/5508723/story.html). Montreal Gazette, Jason Magder, October 6, 2011. .

[2] http://www.datawind.com/

[3] "Meet Aakash, India's $35 'Laptop'" (http://india.blogs.nytimes.com/2011/10/05/meet-aakash-indias-35-laptop/?scp=1&sq=Aakash&st=cse). New York Times, October 5, 2011, Pamposh Raina and Heather Timmons. October 5, 2011. .

[4] "Will Cheap Computer Bridge India's Digital Divide?" (http://www.npr.org/2011/11/02/141944012/will-cheap-computer-bridge-indias-digital-divide?ft=1&f=1001). NPR, Corey Flintoff, November 2, 2011. .

[5] "Aiming for the Other One Billion" (http://india.blogs.nytimes.com/2011/10/06/aiming-for-the-other-one-billion/?scp=4&sq=Aakash&st=cse). New York Times, October 6, 2011, Heather Timmons. October 6, 2011. .

[6] "Biz Briefs: Web on the Run" (http://www.time.com/time/magazine/article/0,9171,1009665,00.html). Time Magazine, Sean Gregory, December 17, 2004. December 17, 2004. .

[7] "Aakash: Why Steve Jobs Would Applaud The World's Cheapest Tablet" (http://www.ibtimes.com/articles/226358/20111006/aakash-steve-jobs-datawind-indian-institute-technology-android-froyo-kapil-sibal-ipad-angry-birds.htm). International Business Times, October 6, 2011, Dave Smith. .

[8] Kurup, Saira (9 Oct., 2011). "'We want to target the billion Indians who are cut off'" (http://timesofindia.indiatimes.com/home/sunday-toi/special-report/We-want-to-target-the-billion-Indians-who-are-cut-off/articleshow/10284832.cms). Times of India. . Retrieved 9 Oct., 2011.

[9] "India Announces World's Cheapest Tablet" (http://blogs.wsj.com/digits/2011/10/05/india-announces-worlds-cheapest-tablet/?KEYWORDS=datawind). India Real Time, viaThe Wall Street Journal, Tripti Lahiri, October 5, 2011. October 5, 2011. .

[10] [bbc_10740817"> (http://www.bbc.co.uk/news/world-south-asia-10740817) "India unveils prototype for $35 touch-screen computer"]. BBC, 23 July 2010. bbc_10740817">.

[11] "India's low-cost tablet is made by Canada's DataWind" (http://www.computerworld.com/s/article/9220554/India_s_low_cost_tablet_is_made_by_Canada_s_DataWind). Computer World, John Ribeiro, October 5, 2011. .

[12] "The $35 Tablet: Will India's 'iPad' Sell Stateside?" (http://www.time.com/time/world/article/0,8599,2097068,00.html). Time Magazine, Nilanjana Bhowmick /Oct. 17, 2011. October 17, 2011. .

[13] "Aakash: We want to target the billion Indians who are cut off, says Suneet Singh Tuli, CEO of Datawind" (http://economictimes.indiatimes.com/opinion/interviews/aakash-we-want-to-target-the-billion-indians-who-are-cut-off-says-suneet-singh-tuli-ceo-of-datawind/articleshow/10286482.cms). Economic Times, October 09, 2011, Saira Kurup. October 9, 2011. .

[14] "India's Low-Cost Tablet is Made By Canada's DataWind" (http://www.cio.com/article/691047/India_s_Low_Cost_Tablet_is_Made_By_Canada_s_DataWind?page=2&taxonomyId=3136 ForceRecrawl: 0). CIO Magazine, John Ribeiro, October 05, 2011. .
[15] "Datawind eyes $500-mn valuation in just 12 mnths" (http://www.business-standard.com/india/news/datawind-eyes-500-mn-valuation-in-just-12-mnths/461695/). Business Standard, Piyali Mandal, January 13, 2012. .
[16] "After "Aakash" DataWind to develop cheapest 4G tablet" (http://www.itpro.in/626725/after-aakash-datawind-to-develop-cheapest-4g-tablet). ITPro India, Priyanka Banerjee, 31 Oct 2011. .
[17] "Impressed by Aakash, Swedish minister to meet Datawind CEO" (http://www.thaindian.com/newsportal/sci-tech/impressed-by-aakash-swedish-minister-to-meet-datawind-ceo_100571226.html). Thaindian News, 18 Oct 2011. .

External links

- Datawind Official Site (http://www.datawind.com/)
- Aakash India website (http://www.aakashindia.co.in/)

GetJar

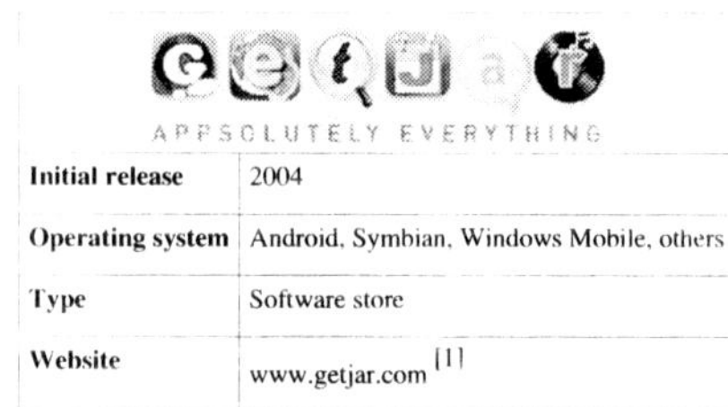

Initial release	2004
Operating system	Android, Symbian, Windows Mobile, others
Type	Software store
Website	www.getjar.com [1]

GetJar is an independent mobile phone application store founded in Lithuania in 2004, with offices in Vilnius, Lithuania and San Mateo, California.[2] [3]

The company provides more than 350,000 mobile applications across major handset platforms including Java ME, BlackBerry, Symbian, Windows Mobile and Android, reaching more than 15 million consumers and has served over 2 billion downloads (2,370,554,782+ Total downloads to date 26 Jan 2012).[4] GetJar allows software developers to upload their applications for free through a developer portal. About 300,000 software developers have used this service resulting in over 1.05 billion downloads.[5] The rate is currently at 3 million downloads per day.[6]

The company was founded by Ilja Laurs in 2004, who remains CEO of the company. Lead investor is Accel Partners.[7]

Awards

- Meffys 2009, "D2C service" winner[8]
- TiECON50 2009, "Wireless" winner[9]
- Mobile Excellence Awards 2009, Best Mobile Service[10]
- On September 1, 2010, the World Economic Forum announced the company as a Technology Pioneer for 2011.[11]

See also

- List of digital distribution platforms for mobile devices

External links

- Official website [1]

References

[1] http://www.getjar.com

[2] (http://www.getjar.com/aboutus/contact) GetJar, contact info, checked on 29th December 2010.

[3] *GetJar: The unknown app store leader* (http://news.cnet.com/8301-30686_3-10392095-266.html), cnews.com

[4] *GetJar offers non-smartphone owners app ability* (http://www.usatoday.com/tech/columnist/edwardbaig/2010-02-11-Baig11_ST_N.htm), USA Today

[5] *GetJar smartphone app shop closes in on a billion downloads* (http://www.independent.co.uk/news/media/getjar-smartphone-app-shop-closes-in-on-a-billion-downloads-1864736.html), The Independent

[6] http://www.mobilebusinessbriefing.com/article/getjar-claims-3m-daily-downloads-names-facebook-as-most-popular-app *GetJar claims 3M daily downloads, names Facebook as most popular app*], GSMA Mpbile Business Briefing

[7] *Mobile Developer Community Site GetJar Gets Funding From Accel* (http://moconews.net/article/419-mobile-developer-community-site-getjar-gets-funding-from-accel/), mocoNews.net

[8] (http://www.meffys.com/about/past-award-winners) Meffys, Past Award Winners, checked on 16th August 2010

[9] (http://www.tie50.net/Winners/Nominations2009.asp) TiECON50, TiE50 2009, checked on 16th August 2010

[10] (http://www.mobilexawards.com/finalists/past/2009/) Mobile Excellence Awards, 2009 Winners & finalists, checked on 16th August 2010

[11] Thirty-One Visionary Companies Selected as Technology Pioneers 2011 (http://www.weforum.org/en/media/Latest News Releases/NR_TP2011)

NDTV

NDTV	
Type	Broadcast, television and online
Country	India
Availability	Nationwide
Founded	by Prannoy Roy in 1988
Headquarters	New Delhi, Delhi, India
Owner	Prannoy Roy Radhika Roy
Key people	Prannoy Roy Radhika Roy Vikram A Chandra Barkha Dutt
Launch date	1988
Former names	New Delhi Television
Picture format	480i (16:9 SDTV) 720p (HDTV)
Official website	[www.ndtv.com www.ndtv.com]

NDTV (BSE: 532529 [1], NSE: NDTV [2]) is an Indian commercial broadcasting television network founded in 1988. It was founded by Prannoy Roy, an eminent journalist and current chairman and director of NDTV Group. NDTV currently has more than 1,000 employees producing news from over twenty locations in India. NDTV is an acronym for the original name of the company, ***New Delhi Television***.[3]

On July 30, 2011, Vikram A Chandra was elevated to the position of group CEO replacing KVL Narayan Rao who is now Executive Vice Chairman of the company.

New Delhi Television is among India's top broadcasters and has twenty-three offices and studios across the country. Its three national news channels NDTV 24x7, NDTV India (Hindi) and NDTV Profit (Business news) form the core of the company. Each year the channel also gives the NDTV Indian of the year awards.

Channels of NDTV Group

Channels of NDTV Group are:

- NDTV 24x7 - English News channel.
- NDTV India - Hindi News channel.
- NDTV Profit - Business News channel.
- NDTV Good Times - Lifestyle channel; JV between NDTV Group and United Breweries Group
- NDTV Hindu- English Chennai Based News Channel, with The Hindu Group

International

- ATN NDTV 24x7
- NDTV Worldwide

Notable personalities

- Vikram A Chandra, Group CEO[4]
- Barkha Dutt[5]
- Pankaj Pachauri (former senior editor of NDTV India, left NDTV to join PMO as Media Advisor)[6]
- Nidhi Kulpati
- Nidhi Razdan
- Sachin Khanna
- Vinod Dua
- Vishnu Som
- Ambika Anand
- Siddharth Vinayak Patankar
- Kamal Khan

Philanthropy & Social Initiatives

NDTV keeps on organising various campaigns through their channels to support Education, Rural Electrification, Awareness on Climate Change. Some of their campaigns are as follows:

- **Greenathon** - It's an event to generate money to spread awareness on climate change and Rural Electrification. It was suppoported by many actors such as Priyanka Chopra, Shah Rukh Khan, Karan Johar. There have been two successful seasons of Greenathon campaign in 2010 and 2011 resuling in donations of more than **5 crore of Rupees**. It is also sponsored by Auto major Toyota.
- **Save Our Tiger Campaign** - This campaign was launched on January 30, 2010 by Indian telecom company Aircel in partnership with NDTV & WWF-India. The goal of this campaign was to create awareness among Indians about the rapidly decreasing tiger population in India. The first year of the NDTV campaign culminated in a 12-hour Telethon. During the telethon, people appealed to political leaders and the masses to do whatever they could to help safeguard the Indian tiger. As a result of the campaign, several prominent political leaders came on air and pledged to protect the forests of their respective states.[7] [8] .During *The Telethon* 19.9 million rupees were raised through donations. The funds collected were donated to "Rapid Response Units [RRU]" to equip and train Forest Departments to respond during emergency situations like man-animal conflict, anti-poaching patrolling, fire-fighting among others.[9]
- **Telethon - Support My School Campaign** - On January 24, 2011 NDTV in partnership with Coca-Cola India, CAF & UN-Habitat lauched "Support My School" campaign. [10] The motive of this campaign was to create awareness on water and sanitation, environment and healthy active living. Indian cricketer Sachin Tendulkar was the brand ambassador of this campaign.[11] On 18 September, 2011 an event was organized to support education

in Rural India. It was supported by Sachin Tendulkar and Bollywood Actor Sanjay Dutt. The event generated more than **7.2 crore Rupees** to fund the needs of more than 140 schools.[12]

- **Fit India Movement** - On March 16, 2011 NDTV & Nirmal Lifestyle launched a long term campaign *Fit India Movement*. The purpose of this movement is to change the way Indians think about their fitness and make India a healthy nation. The "Mission-1" of this movement was "Marks for Sports".[13]
- **Marks for Sports** - This initiative was launched on March 16, 2011 under the "Fit India Movement" of NDTV & Nirmal Lifestyle. The goal of this initiative is to push for inclusion of sports in the school curriculum, hoping that this will make parents encourage their children to take up sports. Actor Ranbir Kapoor, Dr. Prannoy Roy, Chairman, NDTV and Dharmesh Jain, Chairman & MD of Nirmal Lifestyle launched this initiative in New Delhi[14]
- **Save India's Coasts** - This campaign was an initiative of NDTV & Toyota Etios. NDTV's crew traveled the entire coast of India, starting in western Gujarat and ending in West Bengal in 6 weeks, reporting on the issues facing the coast along the way. [15]

Controversies

Allegation of Corruption and Criminal conspiracy

On 20th January, 1998 Central Bureau of Investigation filed cases against New Delhi Television (NDTV) managing director Prannoy Roy, former Director General of Doordarshan R Basu and five other top officials of Doordarshan under Section 120-B of the Indian Penal Code(IPC) for criminal conspiracy and under the Prevention of Corruption Act. According to the CBI charge-sheet, Doordarshan suffered a loss of over Rs 3.52 crore due to the "undue favours" shown to NDTV as its programme The World This Week (TWTW) was put in `A' category instead of `special A' category.[16] [17] [18] [19] [20] [21]

Radia tapes controversy

In November 2010, OPEN magazine carried a story which reported transcripts of some of the telephone conversations of Nira Radia with senior journalists, politicians, and corporate houses, many of whom have denied the allegations. The Central Bureau of Investigation has announced that they have 5,851 recordings of phone conversations by Radia, some of which outline Radia's attempts to broker deals in relation to the 2G spectrum sale.[22] The tapes appear to demonstrate how Radia attempted to use some media persons including NDTV's Barkha Dutt to influence the decision to appoint A. Raja as telecom minister.[23] She always denied her role in this episode with stating her role as simply error of judgment. None of any other news media groups have criticized it very strongly and this is another precise reason to deteriorate acceptance of Media in Indian society. Barkha Dutt is also being investigated by CBI.

Allegation of tax fraud

NDTV, through its foreign subsidiaries, is alleged to have violated Indian tax and corporate laws.[24] NDTV has denied these allegations.

The Sunday Guardian ran a story which exposed the NDTV's financial misdemeanours and malpractices in connivance with ICICI Bank. "NDTV-ICICI loan chicanery saved Roys" [25] provides details of how NDTV's major stake holders raised funds by misdeclaration of the value of shares in NDTV. NDTV has denied the allegations and the NDTV CEO replied [26] to the Sunday Guardian along with the threat of "criminal defamation".

Commonwealth Games Contract

On August 5, 2011 Comptroller and Auditor General of India's report on XIX Commonwealth Games was tabled in Parliament of India. In section 14.4.2 of the report, CAG alleged that while awarding contracts worth Rs 3.78 crore for production & broadcasting of commercials for promoting CWG-2010 to NDTV & CNN-IBN, the Commonwealth Games Organizing Committee followed an arbitrary approach. Proposals were considered in an ad hoc manner, as and when a proposal was received; no form of competitive tendering was adopted. The CAG further said in its report that, "We had no assurance about the competitiveness of the rates quoted by these channels and the need and usefulness of these proposals. From March 2010 to June 2010, the entire pre games publicity and sponsorship publicity was done only on NDTV & CNN-IBN." [27] [28] [29]

References

[1] http://www.bseindia.com/bseplus/StockReach/AdvanceStockReach.aspx?scripcode=532529
[2] http://www.nseindia.com/marketinfo/companyinfo/companysearch.jsp?cons=NDTV§ion=7
[3] "News Delhi TV" (http://members.forbes.com/global/2006/0918/034.html). Forbes.com. . Retrieved 2006-09-18.
[4] "Vikram Chandra" (http://www.ndtv.com/convergence/ndtv/corporatepage/vikram_chandra.aspx). NDTV. .
[5] "Barkha Dutt" (http://www.ndtv.com/page/?type=barkha-statement). NDTV. .
[6] "Pankaj Pachauri" (http://www.thehindu.com/news/national/article2812048.ece). *The Hindu*. .
[7] "Save Our Tiger Campaign" (http://www.wwfindia.org/about_wwf/priority_species/royal_bengal_tiger/what_you_can_do/save_our_tiger_campaign/about/). WWF India. .
[8] "Save Our Tiger" (http://tiger.ndtv.com/aboutourcampaign.aspx). NDTV. .
[9] "Save Our Tiger" (http://tiger.ndtv.com/aboutourcampaign.aspx). NDTV. .
[10] "Support My School Campaign" (http://www.ndtv.com/micro/supportmyschool/aboutthecampaign.aspx). NDTV. .
[11] "Sachin Tendulkar: Joined NDTV "Support My School Campaign"" (http://www.justsachin.com/sachin-tendulkar-news/sachin-tendulkar-joined-ndtv-âsupport-my-school-campaignâ/). .
[12] "Support my school" (http://www.ndtv.com/micro/supportmyschool/default.aspx). NDTV. .
[13] "NDTV-Nirmal Lifestyle launch Marks for Sports under the Fit India movement" (http://www.business-standard.com/india/news/ndtv-nirmal-lifestyle-launch-marks-for-sports-underfit-india-movement/428731/). *Bussiness Standard*. .
[14] "NDTV-Nirmal Lifestyle launch Marks for Sports under the Fit India movement" (http://www.business-standard.com/india/news/ndtv-nirmal-lifestyle-launch-marks-for-sports-underfit-india-movement/428731/). *Bussiness Standard*. .
[15] "Save India's cost" (http://www.ndtv.com/convergence/ndtv/new/Ndtv-Show-Special.aspx?ID=603). NDTV. .
[16] http://zoomindianmedia.wordpress.com/2011/02/14/ndtv-and-prannoy-roy-once-upon-a-time/
[17] http://www.outlookindia.com/article.aspx?204285
[18] http://www.expressindia.com/fe/daily/19980709/19055094.html
[19] http://www.indianexpress.com/ie/daily/19980120/02051164.html
[20] http://www.outlookindia.com/printarticle.aspx?204285
[21] http://www.outlookindia.com/printarticle.aspx?204133
[22] http://www.deccanherald.com/content/116306/radia-tapes-scandal-media.html
[23] http://www.outlookindia.com/article.aspx?268068 The Barkha Dutt & Other Tapes
[24] "NDTV juggles funds, shares abroad, avoids tax" (http://www.sunday-guardian.com/a/1088). The Sunday Guardian. 2010-12-05. . Retrieved 2010-12-06.
[25] http://www.sunday-guardian.com/a/1082
[26] http://www.sunday-guardian.com/a/1083
[27] "CAG Report on XIX Commonwealth Games" (http://saiindia.gov.in/english/home/Our_Products/Audit_Report/Government_Wise/union_audit/recent_reports/union_performance/2011_2012/Civil_ Performance_Audits/Report_No_6_CWG/CWG English - Part-1.pdf). Comptroller & Auditor General of India (Pdf). .
[28] "CAG blames top media houses in Commonwealth Games Scam" (http://www.newsofdelhi.com/featured-post/cag-report-names-ndtvcnn-ibnhindustantimes-in-cwg-scam). *News of Delhi*. .
[29] "Games contracts to media houses arbitrary and biased: CAG" (http://indiatoday.intoday.in/story/games-contracts-to-media-houses-arbitrary-and-biased-cag-report/1/147735.html). *India Today*. .

External links

- Official website (http://http://www.ndtv.com/) (Mobile (http://http://www.ndtv.com/page/mobile-web))
- NDTV (https://twitter.com/ndtv) on Twitter
- NDTV (https://www.facebook.com/ndtv) on Facebook
- ndtv's channel (https://www.youtube.com/user/ndtv) on YouTube
- NDTV Worldwide (http://www.ndtvworldwide.com/)

Subscriber_identity_module

A **subscriber identity module** or **subscriber identification module** (**SIM**) is an integrated circuit that securely stores the International Mobile Subscriber Identity (IMSI) and the related key used to identify and authenticate subscribers on mobile telephony devices (such as mobile phones and computers).

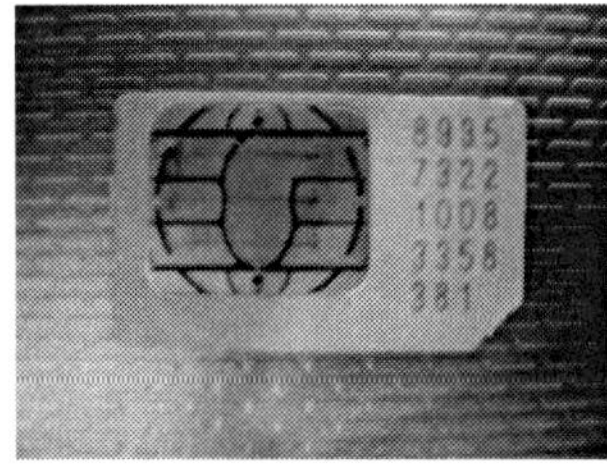

A typical SIM card

A SIM is embedded into a removable *SIM card*, which can be transferred between different mobile devices. SIM cards were first made the same size as a credit card (85.60 mm × 53.98 mm × 0.76 mm). The development of physically-smaller mobile devices prompted the development of a smaller SIM card, the mini-SIM card. Mini-SIM cards have the same thickness as full-size cards, but their length and width are reduced to 25 mm × 15 mm.

A SIM card contains its unique serial number (ICCID), international mobile subscriber identity (IMSI), security authentication and ciphering information, temporary information related to the local network, a list of the services the user has access to and two passwords: a personal identification number (PIN) for ordinary use and a personal unblocking code (PUK) for PIN unlocking.

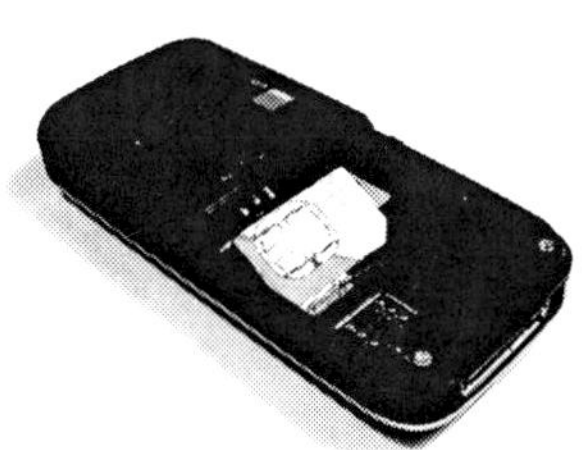

A mini-SIM card next to its electrical contacts in a Nokia 6233

History

The SIM was initially specified by ETSI in the specification with the number TS 11.11. This specification describes the physical and logical behaviour of the SIM. With the development of UMTS the specification work was partially transferred to 3GPP. 3GPP is now responsible for the further development of applications like SIM (TS 51.011) and USIM (TS 31.102) and ETSI for the further development of the physical card UICC.

The first SIM card was made in 1991 by Munich smart-card maker Giesecke & Devrient, who sold the first 300 SIM cards to the Finnish wireless network operator Radiolinja.[1]

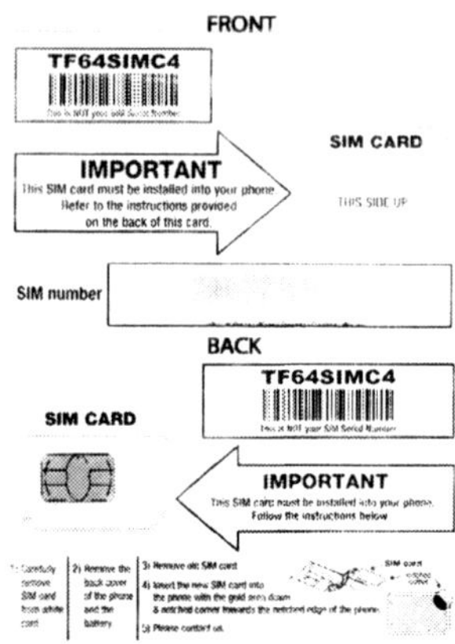

A TracFone Wireless SIM card has no distinctive carrier markings and is only marked as a "SIM CARD"

Design

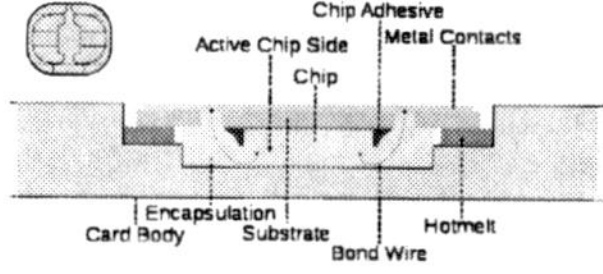

SIM chip structure and packaging

There are three operating voltages for SIM cards: 5 V, 3 V and 1.8 V (ISO/IEC 7816-3 classes A, B and C, respectively). The operating voltage of the majority of SIM cards launched before 1998 was 5 V. SIM cards produced subsequently are compatible with 3 V and 5 V. Modern cards support 5 V, 3 V and 1.8 V.

The microcontrollers used for SIM cards come in different configurations. The typical ROM size is between 64 KB and 512 KB, typical RAM size is between 1 KB and 8 KB, and typical EEPROM size is between 16 KB and 512 KB. The ROM contains the operating system of the card and might contain applets where the EEPROM contains the so called personalisation, which consists of security keys, phone book, SMS settings, etc., and operating system patches.

Modern SIM cards allow that applications can be loaded when the SIM is in use by the subscriber. These applications communicate with the handset or a server using SIM application toolkit, which was initially specified by ETSI in TS 11.14. SIM toolkit applications were initially written in native code using proprietary APIs. In order to allow interoperability of the applications Java Card was taken as the solution of choice by ETSI.

Data

SIM cards store network-specific information used to authenticate and identify subscribers on the network. The most important of these are the ICCID, IMSI, Authentication Key (Ki), Local Area Identity (LAI) and Operator-Specific Emergency Number. The SIM also stores other carrier-specific data such as the SMSC (Short Message Service Center) number, Service Provider Name (SPN), Service Dialing Numbers (SDN), Advice-Of-Charge parameters and Value Added Service (VAS) applications. (Refer to GSM 11.11)

SIM cards can come in at least two capacity types: 32 KB and 64 KB. Both allow a maximum of 250 contacts to be stored on the SIM, but while the 32 KB has room for 33 mobile network codes (MNCs) or "network identifiers", the 64 KB version has room for 80 MNCs. This is used by network operators to store information on preferred networks, mostly used when the SIM is not in its 'home' country but is roaming. The network operator that issued the SIM card can use this to have a SIM card connect to a preferred network in order to make use of the best price and/or quality network instead of having to pay the network operator and accept its quaility the SIM card simply 'saw' first. This does not mean that a SIM card can only connect to a maximum of 33 or 80 networks, this means that the SIM card issuer can only specify up to that amount of preferred networks. if a SIM is outside these preferred networks it will use the first or best available network.

ICCID

Each SIM is internationally identified by its integrated circuit card identifier (ICCID). ICCIDs are stored in the SIM cards and are also engraved or printed on the SIM card body during a process called personalization. The ICCID is defined by the ITU-T recommendation E.118 as the *Primary Account Number*.[2] Its layout is based on ISO/IEC 7812. According to E.118, the number is up to 19 digits long, including a single check digit calculated using the Luhn algorithm. However, the GSM Phase 1[3] defined the ICCID length as 10 octets with operator-specific structure

The number is composed of the following subparts:

Issuer identification number (IIN)

Maximum of seven digits:

- Major industry identifier (MII), 2 fixed digits, 89 for telecommunication purposes.
- Country code, 1-3 digits, as defined by ITU-T recommendation E.164.
- Issuer identifier, 1-4 digits.

Individual account identification

- Individual account identification number. Its length is variable, but every number under one IIN will have the same length.

Check digit

- Single digit calculated from the other digits using the Luhn algorithm.

With the GSM Phase 1 specification using 10 octets into which ICCID is stored as packed BCD, the data field has room for 20 digits with hexadecimal digit "F" being used as filler when necessary.

In practice, this means that on GSM SIM cards there are 20-digit (19+1) and 19-digit (18+1) ICCIDs in use, depending upon the issuer. However, a single issuer always uses the same size for its ICCIDs.

To confuse matters more, SIM factories seem to have varying ways of delivering electronic copies of SIM personalization datasets. Some datasets are without the ICCID checksum digit, others are with the digit.

As required by E.118, The ITU regularly publishes a list of all internationally assigned IIN codes in its Operational Bulletins. The most recent list, as of 23 December, 2011, is in Operational Bulletin No. 971 [4]

International mobile subscriber identity (IMSI)

SIM cards are identified on their individual operator networks by a unique IMSI. Mobile operators connect mobile phone calls and communicate with their market SIM cards using their IMSIs. The format is:

- The first 3 digits represent the Mobile Country Code (MCC).
- The next 2 or 3 digits represent the Mobile Network Code (MNC). 3-digit MNC codes are allowed by E.212 but are mainly used in the United States and Canada.
- The next digits represent the Mobile Subscriber Identification Number (MSIN). Normally there will be 10 digits but would be fewer in the case of a 3-digit MNC or if national regulations indicate that the total length of the IMSI should be less than 15 digits.

Authentication key (K_i)

The K_i is a 128-bit value used in authenticating the SIMs on the mobile network. Each SIM holds a unique K_i assigned to it by the operator during the personalization process. The K_i is also stored in a database (termed authentication center or AuC) on the carrier's network.

The SIM card is designed not to allow the K_i to be obtained using the smart-card interface. Instead, the SIM card provides a function, *Run GSM Algorithm*, that allows the phone to pass data to the SIM card to be signed with the K_i. This, by design, makes usage of the SIM card mandatory unless the K_i can be extracted from the SIM card, or the carrier is willing to reveal the K_i. In practice, the GSM cryptographic algorithm for computing SRES_2 (see step 4, below) from the K_i has certain vulnerabilities[5] that can allow the extraction of the K_i from a SIM card and the making of a duplicate SIM card.

Authentication process:

1. When the Mobile Equipment starts up, it obtains the International Mobile Subscriber Identity (IMSI) from the SIM card, and passes this to the mobile operator requesting access and authentication. The Mobile Equipment may have to pass a PIN to the SIM card before the SIM card will reveal this information.
2. The operator network searches its database for the incoming IMSI and its associated K_i.
3. The operator network then generates a Random Number (RAND, which is a nonce) and signs it with the K_i associated with the IMSI (and stored on the SIM card), computing another number known as Signed Response 1 (SRES_1).
4. The operator network then sends the RAND to the Mobile Equipment, which passes it to the SIM card. The SIM card signs it with its K_i, producing SRES_2, which it gives to the Mobile Equipment along with encryption key K_c. The Mobile Equipment passes SRES_2 on to the operator network.
5. The operator network then compares its computed SRES_1 with the computed SRES_2 that the Mobile Equipment returned. If the two numbers match, the SIM is authenticated and the Mobile Equipment is granted access to the operator's network. K_c is used to encrypt all further communications between the Mobile Equipment and the network.

Location area identity

The SIM stores network state information, which is received from the Location Area Identity (LAI). Operator networks are divided into Location Areas, each having a unique LAI number. When the device changes locations, it stores the new LAI to the SIM and sends it back to the operator network with its new location. If the device is power cycled, it will take data off the SIM, and search for the prior LAI. This saves time by avoiding having to search the whole list of frequencies that the telephone normally would.

SMS messages and contacts

Most SIM cards will orthogonally store a number of SMS messages and phone book contacts. The contacts are stored in simple 'Name and number' pairs: entries containing multiple phone numbers and additional phone numbers will usually not be stored on the SIM card. When a user tries to copy such entries to a SIM the handset's software will break them up into multiple entries, discarding any information that isn't a phone number. The number of contacts and messages stored depends on the SIM; early models would store as few as 5 messages and 20 contacts while modern SIM cards can usually store over 250 contacts.

Formats

SIM cards are available in four standard sizes; full-size, mini-SIM, micro-SIM and embedded SIM. The first to appear was the full-size and is the size of a credit card (85.60 mm × 53.98 mm × 0.76 mm). A newer, more popular, version has the same thickness but has a length of 25 mm and a width of 15 mm, and has one of its corners truncated (chamfered) to prevent misinsertion. The newest incarnation, known as the micro-SIM or 3FF, has dimensions of 15 mm × 12 mm.

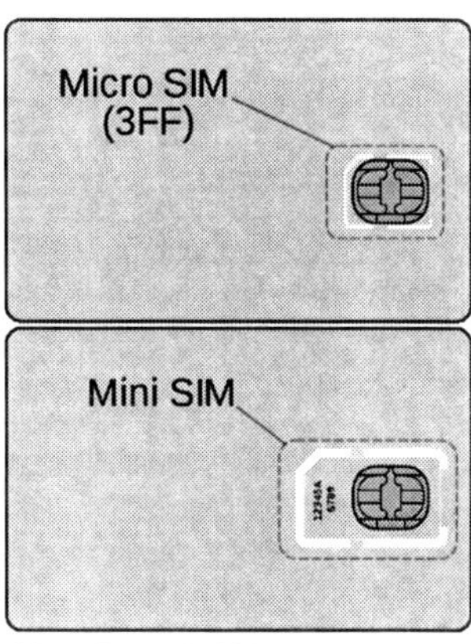

Micro-SIM and mini-SIM, as normally supplied in full-sized carrier cards

The mini-SIM card has the same contact arrangement as the full-size SIM card and is normally supplied within a full-size card carrier, attached by a number of linking pieces. This arrangement (defined in ISO/IEC 7810 as ID-1/000) allows for such a card to be used in a device requiring a full-size card, or to be used in a device requiring a mini-SIM card after cleanly breaking the scorings manufactured in the outline of a mini-SIM card

For use in even smaller devices, the *3FF card* or *micro-SIM* cards have the same thickness and contact arrangements, but the length and width are further reduced to 15 mm × 12 mm.

SIM cards for M2M applications are available in a surface mount SON-8 package which may be soldered directly onto a circuit board.

The logical functions of a SIM card are independent from its format.

Micro-SIM with mini-SIM and full SIM brackets from Telia in Sweden

The memory film from a micro SIM card without the plastic backing plate, next to a US dime, which is approx. 18 mm in diameter.

Embedded SIM from M2M supplier Eseye with an adapter board for evaluation in a Mini-SIM socket

SIM card sizes

SIM card	Standard reference	Length (mm)	Width (mm)	Thickness (mm)
Full-size	ISO/IEC 7810:2003, ID-1	85.60	53.98	0.76
Mini-SIM	ISO/IEC 7810:2003, ID-000	25.00	15.00	0.76
Micro-SIM	ETSI TS 102 221 V9.0.0, Mini-UICC	15.00	12.00	0.76
Embedded-SIM	JEDEC Design Guide 4.8 , SON-8	6.00	5.00	<1.0

The micro-SIM was developed by the European Telecommunications Standards Institute (ETSI) along with SCP, 3GPP (UTRAN/GERAN), 3GPP2 (CDMA2000), ARIB, GSM Association (GSMA SCaG and GSMNA), GlobalPlatform, Liberty Alliance, and the Open Mobile Alliance (OMA) for the purpose of fitting into devices otherwise too small for a mini-SIM card.[6] [7]

The form factor was mentioned in the Dec 1998 3GPP SMG9 UMTS Working Party, which is the standards-setting body for GSM SIM cards,[8] and the form factor was agreed upon in late 2003.[9]

The micro-SIM was created for backward compatibility. The major issue with backward compatibility was the contact area of the chip. Retaining the same contact area allows the micro-SIM to be compatible with the prior, larger SIM readers through the use of plastic cutout surrounds. The SIM was also designed to run at the same speed (5 MHz) as the prior version. The same size and positions of pins resulted in numerous "How-to" tutorials and YouTube video with detailed instructions how to cut a mini-SIM card to micro-SIM size with a sharp knife or scissors. These tutorials became very popular among first owners of iPad 3G after its release on April 30, 2010 and iPhone 4 on June 24, 2010.[10]

The chairman of EP SCP, Dr. Klaus Vedder, said[9]

> "With this decision, we can see that ETSI has responded to a market need from ETSI customers, but additionally there is a strong desire not to invalidate, overnight, the existing interface, nor reduce the performance of the cards. EP SCP expect to finalise the technical realisation for the third form factor at the next SCP plenary meeting, scheduled for February 2004."

The surface mount format provides the same electrical interface as the Full size, 2FF and 3FF SIM cards, but is soldered to the circuit board as part of the manufacturing process. In M2M applications where there is no requirement to change the SIM card, this avoids the requirement for a connector, improving reliability and security.

Developments

When GSM was already in use the specifications were further developed and enhanced with functionality like SMS, GPRS, etc. These development steps are referred as releases by ETSI. Within this development cycles the SIM specification was enhanced as well: new voltage classes, formats and files were introduced.

In GSM-only times the SIM consisted of the hardware and the software. With the advent of UMTS this naming was split: the SIM was now an application and hence only software. The hardware part was called UICC. This split was necessary because UMTS introduced a new application, the USIM. The USIM brought among other things security improvements like the mutual authentication and longer encryption keys and an improved address book.

"SIM cards" in developed countries are today usually UICCs containing at least a SIM and a USIM application. This configuration is necessary because older GSM only handsets are solely compatible with the SIM [application] and some UMTS security enhancements do rely on the USIM [application].

The equivalent of SIM on CDMA networks is CSIM.

A *virtual SIM* is a mobile phone number provided by a mobile network operator that does not require a SIM card to connect phone calls to a user's mobile phone.

Usage in mobile phone standards

The use of SIM cards is mandatory in GSM devices.

The satellite phone networks Iridium, Thuraya and Inmarsat's BGAN also use SIM cards. Sometimes these SIM cards work in regular GSM phones and also allow GSM customers to roam in satellite networks by using their own SIM card in a satellite phone.

SIM card for Thuraya satellite phone

Japan's 2G PDC system (which will be completely shut down by 2012; SoftBank Mobile has already shut down PDC from March 31, 2010) also specifies a SIM, but this has never been implemented commercially. The specification of the interface between the Mobile Equipment and the SIM is given in the RCR STD-27 annex 4. The Subscriber Identity Module Expert Group was a committee of specialists assembled by the European Telecommunications Standards Institute (ETSI) to draw up the specifications (GSM 11.11) for interfacing between smart cards and mobile telephones. In 1994, the name SIMEG was changed to SMG9.

Grameenphone's SIM card

Japan's current and next generation cellular systems are based on W-CDMA (UMTS) and CDMA2000 and all use SIM cards.

CDMA-based devices originally did not use a removable card, and the service for these phones bound to a unique identifier contained in the handset itself. This is most prevalent in operators in the Americas. The first publication of the TIA-820 standard (also known as 3GPP2 C.S0023) in 2000 defined the Removable User Identity Module (R-UIM). Card-based CDMA devices are most prevalent in Asia.

The equivalent of a SIM in UMTS is called the Universal Integrated Circuit Card (UICC), which runs a USIM application. The UICC is still colloquially called a *SIM card*.

KDDI's au IC-Card

SIM and carriers

The SIM card introduced a new and significant business opportunity of mobile telecommunications operator/carrier business of the mobile virtual network operator (MVNO) which does not own or operate a cellular telecoms network, but which leases capacity from one of the network operators, and only provides a SIM card to its customers. MVNOs first appeared in Denmark, Hong Kong, Finland and the UK and today exist in over 50 countries, including most of Europe, United States, Canada, Australia and parts of Asia, and account for approximately 10% of all mobile phone subscribers around the world.

On some networks, the mobile phone is locked to its carrier SIM card, meaning that only the specific carrier's SIM cards will work. This is more common in markets where mobile phones are heavily subsidised by the carriers, and the business model depends on the customer staying with the service provider for a minimum term (typically 12 or 24 months). Common examples are the GSM networks in the United States, Canada, Australia, the UK and Poland. Many businesses offer the ability to remove the SIM lock from a phone, effectively making it possible to then use the phone on any network by inserting a different SIM card. Mostly, GSM and 3G mobile handsets can easily be unlocked and used on any suitable network with any SIM card.

In countries where the phones are not subsidised, *e.g.*, Italy, India and Belgium, all phones are unlocked. Where the phone is not locked to its SIM card, the users can easily switch networks by simply replacing the SIM card of one network with that of another while using only one phone. This is typical, for example, among users who may want to optimise their carrier's traffic by different tariffs to different friends on different networks, or when traveling internationally.

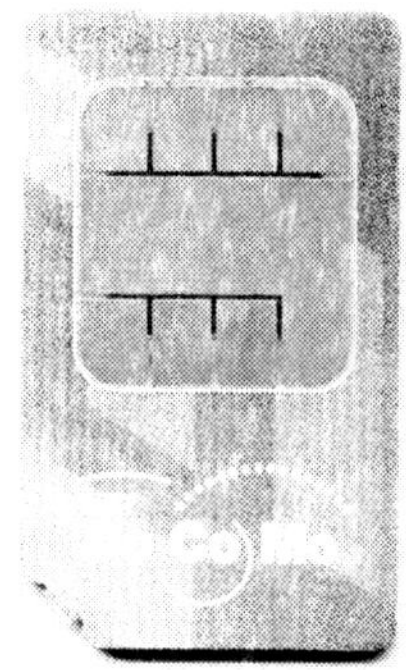

NTT DoCoMo's FOMA Card

SIMware

A term used to describe software held on or running on a SIM card.[11]

See also

- International Mobile Equipment Identity (IMEI)
- GSM 03.48
- SIM cloning
- SIM connector
- IP Multimedia Services Identity Module (ISIM)
- W-SIM (Willcom-SIM)
- Mobile equipment identifier (MEID)
- VMAC
- Mobile signature
- Single Wire Protocol (SWP)
- SIM Application Toolkit (STK)
- Mobile broadband
- Tethering
- Smart card

References

[1] History of Giesecke & Devrient (http://www.gi-de.com/portal/page?_pageid=44,62528&_dad=portal&_schema=PORTAL)

[2] ITU-T, ITU-T Recommendation E.118, The international telecommunication charge card, Revision history (http://www.itu.int/rec/T-REC-E.118), Revision "05/2006" (http://www.itu.int/rec/dologin_pub.asp?lang=e&id=T-REC-E.118-200605-I!!PDF-E&type=items)

[3] ETSI, ETSI Recommendation GSM 11.11, Specifications of the SIM-ME Interface, Version 3.16.0 (http://www.3gpp.org/ftp/Specs/archive/11_series/11.11/1111-3G0.ZIP)

[4] http://www.itu.int/pub/T-SP-OB.971-2011

[5] "Hackers crack open mobile network" (http://www.bbc.co.uk/news/technology-13013577). *31 December 2010* (bbc.co.uk). 20 April 2011. . Retrieved 13 August 2011.

[6] Gaby Lenhart, Project leader: ETSI Technical Committee Smart Card Platform (TB SCP) (2006-04-01). "The Smart Card Platform" (http://docbox.etsi.org//Workshop/2006/Salud Mexico/Gaby Lenhart - CENETEC_2006_04.ppt). ETSI Technical Committee Smart Card Platform (TB SCP). . Retrieved 30 January 2010. "SCP is co-operating on both technical and service aspects with a number of other committees both within and outside the telecommunications sector."

[7] Segan, Sascha (2010-01-27). "Inside the iPad Lurks the 'Micro SIM'" (http://www.pcmag.com/article2/0,2817,2358489,00.asp). PC Magazine. . Retrieved 30 January 2010.

[8] "DRAFT Report of the SMG9 UMTS Working Party, meeting #7 hosted by Nokia in Copenhagen, 15.-16- December 1998" (http://www.3gpp.org/ftp/TSG_T/WG3_USIM/TSGT3_01/docs/t3-99003.pdf). *3GPP*. 25 January 1999. . Retrieved 27 January 2010. "One manufacturer stated that it may be difficult to meeting ISO mechanical standards for a combined ID-1/micro-SIM card."

[9] Antipolis, Sophia (2003-12-08). "New form factor for smart cards introduced" (http://www.smartcardstrends.com/det_atc.php?idu=287). SmartCard Trends. . Retrieved 30 January 2010. "The work item for the so-called Third Form Factor, "3FF", was agreed, after intensive discussions, at the SCP meeting held last week in London."

[10] "How to make MicroSIM" (http://www.youtube.com/watch?v=6B0G_qjebJY). .

[11] "Case details for Trade Mark 2516989" (http://www.ipo.gov.uk/domestic?domesticnum=2516989), Intellectual Property Office (UK)

Further reading

- Sim Card Cloning (http://www.5ne.org/sim-cloning)

External links

- ETSI Smart Card standards (102 221) (http://pda.etsi.org/pda/AQuery.asp?qSEARCH_STRING=102+221&qSEARCH_Type=EXACT&submit1=Search&qNB_TO_DISPLAY=10&qOFFSET=0&qSORT=DEFAULT)
- GSM 11.11 (http://www.3gpp.org/ftp/specs/html-info/1111.htm) - Specification of the Subscriber Identity Module — Mobile Equipment (SIM — ME) interface.
- GSM 11.14 (http://www.3gpp.org/ftp/specs/html-info/1114.htm) - Specification of the SIM Application Toolkit for the Subscriber Identity Module — Mobile Equipment (SIM — ME) interface
- GSM 03.48 (http://www.3gpp.org/ftp/specs/html-info/0348.htm) - Specification of the security mechanisms for SIM application toolkit.
- GSM 03.48 Java API (http://gsm0348.googlecode.com) - API and realization of GSM 03.48 in Java.
- ITU-T E.118 (http://www.itu.int/rec/T-REC-E.118-200605-I/en) - The International Telecommunication Charge Card. 2006 ITU-T.

2G

2G (or **2-G**) is short for second-generation wireless telephone technology. Second generation 2G cellular telecom networks were commercially launched on the GSM standard in Finland by Radiolinja (now part of Elisa Oyj) in 1991.[1] Three primary benefits of 2G networks over their predecessors were that phone conversations were digitally encrypted; 2G systems were significantly more efficient on the spectrum allowing for far greater mobile phone penetration levels; and 2G introduced data services for mobile, starting with SMS text messages.

After 2G was launched, the previous mobile telephone systems were retrospectively dubbed 1G. While radio signals on 1G networks are analog, radio signals on 2G networks are digital. Both systems use digital signaling to connect the radio towers (which listen to the handsets) to the rest of the telephone system.

2G has been superseded by newer technologies such as 2.5G, 2.75G, 3G, and 4G; however, 2G networks are still used in many parts of the world.

2G technologies

2G technologies can be divided into TDMA-based and CDMA-based standards depending on the type of multiplexing used. The main 2G standards are:

- GSM (TDMA-based), originally from Europe but used in almost all countries on all six inhabited continents. Today accounts for over 80% of all subscribers around the world. Over 60 GSM operators are also using CDMA2000 in the 450 MHz frequency band (CDMA450).[2]
- IS-95 *aka* cdmaOne (CDMA-based, commonly referred as simply CDMA in the US), used in the Americas and parts of Asia. Today accounts for about 17% of all subscribers globally. Over a dozen CDMA operators have migrated to GSM including operators in Mexico, India, Australia and South Korea.
- PDC (TDMA-based), used exclusively in Japan
- iDEN (TDMA-based), proprietary network used by Nextel in the United States and Telus Mobility in Canada
- IS-136 a.k.a. D-AMPS (TDMA-based, commonly referred as simply 'TDMA' in the US), was once prevalent in the Americas but most have migrated to GSM.

2G services are frequently referred as Personal Communications Service, or PCS, in the United States.

Capacities, advantages, and disadvantages

Capacity

Using digital signals between the handsets and the towers increases system capacity in two key ways:

- Digital voice data can be compressed and multiplexed much more effectively than analog voice encodings through the use of various codecs, allowing more calls to be packed into the same amount of radio bandwidth.
- The digital systems were designed to emit less radio power from the handsets. This meant that cells had to be smaller, so more cells had to be placed in the same amount of space. This was made possible by cell towers and related equipment getting less expensive.

Advantages

- The lower power emissions helped address health concerns.
- Going all-digital allowed for the introduction of digital data services, such as SMS and email.
- Greatly reduced fraud. With analog systems it was possible to have two or more "cloned" handsets that had the same phone number.
- Enhanced privacy. A key digital advantage not often mentioned is that digital cellular calls are much harder to eavesdrop on by use of radio scanners. While the security algorithms used have proved not to be as secure as initially advertised, 2G phones are immensely more private than 1G phones, which have no protection against eavesdropping.

Disadvantages

- In less populous areas, the weaker digital signal may not be sufficient to reach a cell tower. This tends to be a particular problem on 2G systems deployed on higher frequencies, but is mostly not a problem on 2G systems deployed on lower frequencies. National regulations differ greatly among countries which dictate where 2G can be deployed.
- Analog has a smooth decay curve, digital a jagged steppy one. This can be both an advantage and a disadvantage. Under good conditions, digital will sound better. Under slightly worse conditions, analog will experience static, while digital has occasional dropouts. As conditions worsen, though, digital will start to completely fail, by dropping calls or being unintelligible, while analog slowly gets worse, generally holding a call longer and allowing at least a few words to get through.
- While digital calls tend to be free of static and background noise, the lossy compression used by the codecs takes a toll; the range of sound that they convey is reduced. You will hear less of the tonality of someone's voice talking on a digital cellphone, but you will hear it more clearly.

Evolution

2G networks were built mainly for voice services and slow data transmission.

Some protocols, such as EDGE for GSM and 1x-RTT for CDMA2000, are defined as "3G" services (because they are defined in IMT-2000 specification documents), but are considered by the general public to be 2.5G or 2.75G services because they are several times slower than present-day 3G service.

2.5G (GPRS)

2.5G ("**second and a half generation**") is used to describe 2G-systems that have implemented a packet-switched domain in addition to the circuit-switched domain. It does not necessarily provide faster services because bundling of timeslots is used for circuit-switched data services (HSCSD) as well.

The first major step in the evolution of GSM networks to 3G occurred with the introduction of General Packet Radio Service (GPRS). CDMA2000 networks similarly evolved through the introduction of 1xRTT. The combination of these capabilities came to be known as 2.5G.

GPRS could provide data rates from 56 kbit/s up to 115 kbit/s. It can be used for services such as Wireless Application Protocol (WAP) access, Multimedia Messaging Service (MMS), and for Internet communication services such as email and World Wide Web access. GPRS data transfer is typically charged per megabyte of traffic transferred, while data communication via traditional circuit switching is billed per minute of connection time, independent of whether the user actually is utilizing the capacity or is in an idle state.

1xRTT supports bi-directional (up and downlink) peak data rates up to 153.6 kbit/s, delivering an average user data throughput of 80-100 kbit/s in commercial networks.[3] It can also be used for WAP, SMS & MMS services, as well as Internet access.

2.75G (EDGE)

GPRS1 networks evolved to EDGE networks with the introduction of 8PSK encoding. Enhanced Data rates for GSM Evolution (EDGE), Enhanced GPRS (EGPRS), or IMT Single Carrier (IMT-SC) is a backward-compatible digital mobile phone technology that allows improved data transmission rates, as an extension on top of standard GSM. EDGE was deployed on GSM networks beginning in 2003—initially by Cingular (now AT&T) in the United States.

EDGE is standardized by 3GPP as part of the GSM family and it is an upgrade that provides a potential three-fold increase in capacity of GSM/GPRS networks. The specification achieves higher data-rates (up to 236.8 kbit/s) by switching to more sophisticated methods of coding (8PSK), within existing GSM timeslots.

See also

- Mobile radio telephone, also known as *0G*
- 1G
- 3G
- 4G
- 2G spectrum scam, India

References

[1] "Radiolinja's History" (http://www.elisa.com/english/index.cfm?t=6&o=6532.50). April 20, 2004. . Retrieved December 23, 2009.
[2] "CDMA Worldwide" (http://www.cdg.org/worldwide/index.asp?h_area=0&h_technology=999&h_frequency=1). . Retrieved December 23, 2009.
[3] "CDMA2000 1X" (http://www.cdg.org/technology/cdma20001x.asp). *CDG.org*. CDMA Development Group. . Retrieved July 31, 2011.

General_Packet_Radio_Service

General packet radio service (GPRS) is a packet oriented mobile data service on the 2G and 3G cellular communication system's global system for mobile communications (GSM). GPRS was originally standardized by European Telecommunications Standards Institute (ETSI) in response to the earlier CDPD and i-mode packet-switched cellular technologies. It is now maintained by the 3rd Generation Partnership Project (3GPP).[1] [2]

GPRS usage is typically charged based on volume of data. This contrasts with circuit switching data, which is typically billed per minute of connection time, regardless of whether or not the user transfers data during that period.

GPRS data is typically supplied either as part of a bundle (e.g., 5 GB per month for a fixed fee) or on a pay-as-you-use basis. Usage above the bundle cap is either charged per megabyte or disallowed. The pay-as-you-use charging is typically per megabyte of traffic.

GPRS is a best-effort service, implying variable throughput and latency that depend on the number of other users sharing the service concurrently, as opposed to circuit switching, where a certain quality of service (QoS) is guaranteed during the connection. In 2G systems, GPRS provides data rates of 56–114 kbit/second.[3] 2G cellular technology combined with GPRS is sometimes described as *2.5G*, that is, a technology between the second (2G) and third (3G) generations of mobile telephony.[4] It provides moderate-speed data transfer, by using unused time division multiple access (TDMA) channels in, for example, the GSM system. GPRS is integrated into GSM Release 97 and newer releases.

Technical overview

The GPRS core network allows 2G, 3G and WCDMA mobile networks to transmit IP packets to external networks such as the Internet. The GPRS system is an integrated part of the GSM network switching subsystem.

Services offered

GPRS extends the GSM Packet circuit switched data capabilities and makes the following services possible:

- SMS messaging and broadcasting
- "Always on" internet access
- Multimedia messaging service (MMS)
- Push to talk over cellular (PoC)
- Instant messaging and presence—wireless village
- Internet applications for smart devices through wireless application protocol (WAP)
- Point-to-point (P2P) service: inter-networking with the Internet (IP)
- Point-to-Multipoint (P2M) service: point-to-multipoint multicast and point-to-multipoint group calls

If SMS over GPRS is used, an SMS transmission speed of about 30 SMS messages per minute may be achieved. This is much faster than using the ordinary SMS over GSM, whose SMS transmission speed is about 6 to 10 SMS messages per minute.

Protocols supported

GPRS supports the following protocols:

- Internet protocol (IP). In practice, built-in mobile browsers use IPv4 since IPv6 was not yet popular.
- Point-to-point protocol (PPP). In this mode PPP is often not supported by the mobile phone operator but if the mobile is used as a modem to the connected computer, PPP is used to tunnel IP to the phone. This allows an IP address to be assigned dynamically to the mobile equipment.
- X.25 connections. This is typically used for applications like wireless payment terminals, although it has been removed from the standard. X.25 can still be supported over PPP, or even over IP, but doing this requires either a network based router to perform encapsulation or intelligence built in to the end-device/terminal; e.g., user equipment (UE).

When TCP/IP is used, each phone can have one or more IP addresses allocated. GPRS will store and forward the IP packets to the phone even during handover. The TCP handles any packet loss (e.g. due to a radio noise induced pause).

Hardware

Devices supporting GPRS are divided into three classes:

Class A

Can be connected to GPRS service and GSM service (voice, SMS), using both at the same time. Such devices are known to be available today.

Class B

Can be connected to GPRS service and GSM service (voice, SMS), but using only one or the other at a given time. During GSM service (voice call or SMS), GPRS service is suspended, and then resumed automatically after the GSM service (voice call or SMS) has concluded. Most GPRS mobile devices are Class B.

Class C

Are connected to either GPRS service or GSM service (voice, SMS). Must be switched manually between one or the other service.

A true Class A device may be required to transmit on two different frequencies at the same time, and thus will need two radios. To get around this expensive requirement, a GPRS mobile may implement the dual transfer mode (DTM) feature. A DTM-capable mobile may use simultaneous voice and packet data, with the network coordinating to ensure that it is not required to transmit on two different frequencies at the same time. Such mobiles are considered pseudo-Class A, sometimes referred to as "simple class A". Some networks support DTM since 2007.

USB 3G/GPRS modems use a terminal-like interface over USB 1.1, 2.0 and later, data formats V.42bis, and RFC 1144 and some models have connector for external antenna. Modems can be added as cards (for laptops) or external USB devices which are similar in shape and size to a computer mouse, or nowadays more like a pendrive.

Huawei E220 3G/GPRS Modem

Addressing

A GPRS connection is established by reference to its access point name (APN). The APN defines the services such as wireless application protocol (WAP) access, short message service (SMS), multimedia messaging service (MMS), and for Internet communication services such as email and World Wide Web access.

In order to set up a GPRS connection for a wireless modem, a user must specify an APN, optionally a user name and password, and very rarely an IP address, all provided by the network operator.

Coding schemes and speeds

The upload and download speeds that can be achieved in GPRS depend on a number of factors such as:

- the number of BTS TDMA time slots assigned by the operator
- the channel encoding used.
- the maximum capability of the mobile device expressed as a GPRS multislot class

Multiple access schemes

The multiple access methods used in GSM with GPRS are based on frequency division duplex (FDD) and TDMA. During a session, a user is assigned to one pair of up-link and down-link frequency channels. This is combined with time domain statistical multiplexing; i.e., packet mode communication, which makes it possible for several users to share the same frequency channel. The packets have constant length, corresponding to a GSM time slot. The down-link uses first-come first-served packet scheduling, while the up-link uses a scheme very similar to reservation ALOHA (R-ALOHA). This means that slotted ALOHA (S-ALOHA) is used for reservation inquiries during a contention phase, and then the actual data is transferred using dynamic TDMA with first-come first-served scheduling.

Channel encoding

Channel encoding is based on a convolutional code at different code rates and GMSK modulation defined for GSM. The following table summarises the options:

Coding scheme	Speed (kbit/s)
CS-1	8.0
CS-2	12.0
CS-3	14.4
CS-4	20.0

The least robust, but fastest, coding scheme (CS-4) is available near a base transceiver station (BTS), while the most robust coding scheme (CS-1) is used when the mobile station (MS) is further away from a BTS.

Using the CS-4 it is possible to achieve a user speed of 20.0 kbit/s per time slot. However, using this scheme the cell coverage is 25% of normal. CS-1 can achieve a user speed of only 8.0 kbit/s per time slot, but has 98% of normal coverage. Newer network equipment can adapt the transfer speed automatically depending on the mobile location.

In addition to GPRS, there are two other GSM technologies which deliver data services: circuit-switched data (CSD) and high-speed circuit-switched data (HSCSD). In contrast to the shared nature of GPRS, these instead establish a dedicated circuit (usually billed per minute). Some applications such as video calling may prefer HSCSD, especially when there is a continuous flow of data between the endpoints.

The following table summarises some possible configurations of GPRS and circuit switched data services.

Technology	Download (kbit/s)	Upload (kbit/s)	TDMA Timeslots allocated (DL+UL)
CSD	9.6	9.6	1+1
HSCSD	28.8	14.4	2+1
HSCSD	43.2	14.4	3+1
GPRS	80.0	20.0 (Class 8 & 10 and CS-4)	4+1
GPRS	60.0	40.0 (Class 10 and CS-4)	3+2
EGPRS (EDGE)	236.8	59.2 (Class 8, 10 and MCS-9)	4+1
EGPRS (EDGE)	177.6	118.4 (Class 10 and MCS-9)	3+2

Multislot Class

The multislot class determines the speed of data transfer available in the Uplink and Downlink directions. It is a value between 1 to 45 which the network uses to allocate radio channels in the uplink and downlink direction. Multislot class with values greater than 31 are referred to as high multislot classes.

A multislot allocation is represented as, for example, 5+2. The first number is the number of downlink timeslots and the second is the number of uplink timeslots allocated for use by the mobile station. A commonly used value is class 10 for many GPRS/EGPRS mobiles which uses a maximum of 4 timeslots in downlink direction and 2 timeslots in uplink direction. However simultaneously a maximum number of 5 simultaneous timeslots can be used in both uplink and downlink. The network will automatically configure the for either 3+2 or 4+1 operation depending on the nature of data transfer.

Some high end mobiles, usually also supporting UMTS also support GPRS/EDGE multislot class 32. According to 3GPP TS 45.002 (Release 6), Table B.2, mobile stations of this class support 5 timeslots in downlink and 3 timeslots in uplink with a maximum number of 6 simultaneously used timeslots. If data traffic is concentrated in downlink direction the network will configure the connection for 5+1 operation. When more data is transferred in the uplink the network can at any time change the constellation to 4+2 or 3+3. Under the best reception conditions, i.e. when the best EDGE modulation and coding scheme can be used, 5 timeslots can carry a bandwidth of 5*59.2 kbit/s = 296 kbit/s. In uplink direction, 3 timeslots can carry a bandwidth of 3*59.2 kbit/s = 177.6 kbit/s.[5]

Multislot Classes for GPRS/EGPRS

Multislot Class	Downlink TS	Uplink TS	Active TS
1	1	1	2
2	2	1	3
3	2	2	3
4	3	1	4
5	2	2	4
6	3	2	4
7	3	3	4
8	4	1	5
9	3	2	5
10	4	2	5
11	4	3	5
12	4	4	5
30	5	1	6
31	5	2	6
32	5	3	6
33	5	4	6
34	5	5	6

•

Attributes of a multislot class

Each multislot class identifies the following:

- the maximum number of Timeslots that can be allocated on uplink
- the maximum number of Timeslots that can be allocated on downlink
- the total number of timeslots which can be allocated by the network to the mobile
- the time needed for the MS to perform adjacent cell signal level measurement and get ready to transmit
- the time needed for the MS to get ready to transmit
- the time needed for the MS to perform adjacent cell signal level measurement and get ready to receive
- the time needed for the MS to get ready to receive.

The different multislot class specification is detailed in the Annex B of the 3GPP Technical Specification 45.002 (Multiplexing and multiple access on the radio path)

Usability

The maximum speed of a GPRS connection offered in 2003 was similar to a modem connection in an analog wire telephone network, about 32-40 kbit/s, depending on the phone used. Latency is very high; round-trip time (RTT) is typically about 600-700 ms and often reaches 1 s. GPRS is typically prioritized lower than speech, and thus the quality of connection varies greatly.

Devices with latency/RTT improvements (via, for example, the extended UL TBF mode feature) are generally available. Also, network upgrades of features are available with certain operators. With these enhancements the active round-trip time can be reduced, resulting in significant increase in application-level throughput speeds.

See also

- Code division multiple access (CDMA)
- Enhanced data rates for GSM evolution (EDGE)
- Universal mobile telephone system (UMTS)
- GPRS core network
- Sub-network dependent convergence protocol (SNDCP)
- IP Multimedia Subsystem
- High-speed downlink packet access (HSDPA)
- Cellular data communication protocol
- List of device bandwidths

References

[1] ETSI (http://www.etsi.org/WebSite/homepage.aspx)
[2] http://www.3gpp.org/3GPP
[3] General packet radio service from Qkport (http://about.qkport.com/g/general_packet_radio_service)
[4] Mobile Phone Generations from (http://www.funsms.net/mobile_phone_generations.htm)
[5] http://mobilesociety.typepad.com/mobile_life/2007/04/gprs_and_edge_m.html

External links

- 3GPP AT command set for user equipment (UE) (http://www.3gpp.org/ftp/Specs/latest/Rel-8/27_series/27007-841.zip)
- GPRS security information (archive.org) (http://web.archive.org/web/20080209213430/http://www.gprssecurity.com/)
- Free GPRS resources (http://www.telecomspace.com/datatech-gprs.html)
- Free online tutorial (http://www.comsoc.org/livepubs/surveys/public/3q99issue/bettstetter.html).
- GSM World, the trade association for GSM and GPRS network operators (http://www.gsmworld.com/technology/gprs/intro.shtml).
- Palowireless GPRS resource center (http://www.palowireless.com/gprs/)
- GPRS attach and PDP context activation sequence diagram (http://www.eventhelix.com/RealtimeMantra/Telecom/gprs_attach_pdp_sequence_diagram.pdf)

Article Sources and Contributors

Aakash_(tablet) *Source*: http://en.wikipedia.org/w/index.php?title=Aakash_%28tablet%29 *Contributors*: 06baraxs, 220 of Borg, 7ishantg, 842U, AakashTablet, Abdul raja, Abhijeetjha0, Abhis2.0, Abhishek.1722012, Abhishikt, Adinasa, Alex E. Clarke, Alexf, Amigosujo, Anaxial, AndrewHowse, Aravind.iitr, Arnavchaudhary, Arun K Sivanandan, AshLin, Beao, Ben Ben, Bobbystephen, Brianski, Cb6, Clovis Sangrail, Coercorash, CommonsDelinker, Composemi, Crampal, Deeuubee, Derekkopke, Dialectric, Dileepgjacob, Dinakarr, Download, Dsvyas, Error, Eugene-elgato, Fanatix, Fayenatic london, Frap, Fxd25, Gdandona, Geniac, Ghostinthebox, Grundle2600, Gunrajsm, H2hhelp, Haseo9999, Hethrir, Infinite dreams9586, Jac16888, Jeddufff, Jerryobject, Jim1138, Johnxxx9, K7.india, Karthikndr, Kkm010, Kshitijagrwl, Learnomlette, LeeColleton, Lightmouse, Lucian303, MSoderling, Mahjongg, MarQ, Marcus Qwertyus, Mastertushar, Materialscientist, Meco, Meetsangvikar, Modernrectifier, Nafhan, Nareshguptaks, NeOFreedom, Neo-Jay, Nirala nagar, Nitish.game, Ohconfucius, Pacey2007, Parshant dewan, PatheticCopyEditor, Pol098, Prajapatimishra, Prannoymathew7, Prashantsultania, Prd.ban, Pteek, Racklever, Rahuln1988, Rahulpattuvam, Rajendra bn, RaviC, Rawsun, Rcsprinter123, RobertMfromLI, Robofish, Roland zh, Rsrikanth05, RudolfRed, SF007, Sainath468, Sairameshpsr, Sbmeirow, Shrish, Skvnet, Swift&silent, Taxman, Techman224, TexMurphy, Tgeairn, Tom Worthington, Trunks ishida, Trusilver, TutterMouse, Tyson567, Utcursch, Veryhuman, Vibhor5000, Vipinhari, Virtualage, Volatileacid, Wayfarerz, Wikieditorin, Wikiklrsc, Wtanaka, Wuffyz, 356 anonymous edits

Android_(operating_system) *Source*: http://en.wikipedia.org/w/index.php?title=Android_%28operating_system%29 *Contributors*: 336, 777sms, 9th jinchuriki, A bit iffy, A.sutton, A520, A5b, A665321, Aadadurov, Abhishek191288, Abledsoe78, Abrahami, Aceleo, Acery, Adambiswanger1, Adamjacobd, Adamwatters, Adi19956, Adileader, AdjustablePliers, Adm.Wiggin, Afriza, Aftekology, Aftershave, Agentlame, Akbarzpro, Akshayjain123, AladdinSE, Alboran, Alejo2083, Alex, AlexKucherenko, AlexMS, Alexey Izbyshev, Alexius08, Alfstar1997, Ali'i, Aliendude5300, Alisha.4m, AlistairMcMillan, Allen Moore, Allstarecho, Alunphillips, Alvestrand, Amarenderjannu, Amatulic, Ambictus, Amckern, Ameliorate!, Ancheta Wis, Andareed, Anderssl, Andreas Bischoff, Andreas Carter, Andrejavus, Andresfi, Andrew Delong, AndrewHowse, Andrewkantor, Androidliscence, Androidmids, Andyjsmith, Anindya Bakshi, Ankitasdeveloper, AnonMoos, Anoopan, Anoopmichael, Anthonynon, Antnee, Aoeuser, Apobilgin, Aquarat, Aradius, Aranci, Arc Orion, Arcanis, Archangelsk, ArgetlahmSource, Arghya139, Arichnad, Arjun G. Menon, ArthasO1, Aryamanjain, Aryndar, Ash Crow, Ashishjain999, Ashwin18, Astonmartini, Asymmetric, Athzai Khaine, Atlantia, AtteL, Attilios, Audi152, Audriusa, Automate, AwamerT, Axl, Ayd00, Ayd000, Ayd86, Aydceri, Aydcery00, Aydcery86, Aydchery00, Aydin00, BY.Apps, Bagelfat101010, Bahua, Bangbang.S, Banksbr2, Barek, Barte, Bayonetblaha, Bbaumer, Bbisgard, Bdesham, Bedna, Beland, Bender235, Benjaminb, Benlisquare, Berelv, Betmenko, Bevo, Bhny, Bilbo571, Binarybits, Bios Element, Blackfireshocker, Blahbabe61, Blindwaves, Blogfactor, Blowdart, Bmwtroll, Bomazi, Bonadea, Bosqueschool, Bovineone, Bpave777, Brandorr, Brianreading, Brianski, Briantist, Bryan.burgers, BucsWeb, Bungalowbill, Bweono, C628, CCalo, CJLL Wright, CJMiller, CPGustafson511, CRGreathouse, Cacophony, Caltas, Can't sleep, clown will eat me, CaribDigita, Carlton.northern, Carrlos, CaseyBorders, CastAStone, Causa sui, Cbmaster, Cbr1000f, Cburnett, Ch Th Jo, Chainz, Chancer1001, ChaosData, Chardot, Charles.h.white@gmail.com, CharlesC, Cheekeong123, Cherie327, Cherkash, Chezi-Schlaff, Chiles Malesters, Chillpenguin, Chillum, Chirags, Chr1syr, Chris Bainbridge, Chris the speller, Chris.p.wu, ChrisHeller, Chrismiceli, Chrispilot2293, Christian75, Ciphergoth, Ciphers, ClaudeReigns, Clovis Sangrail, Coffee, CommonsDelinker, ComputerGeek706, Conan, Conti, Conzorz, Coolbho3000, Coolstoryhansel, CoordinateFreak, Corevette, Costa Discordia, Count Chockula, Cpl Syx, CrabbyPatrick, Crackerspeanut12, Craigbarnes85, Craigbrass, Cresdajv, Crysb, Csrempert, Ctjf83, Cybercobra, Cyrotux, D-Notice, D20sheets, DGMDGM, DHN, DStoykov, Daabomb, Daev, Dale Arnett, Dancter, Dandyandroid, Danger, Daniel.Cardenas, DanielPharos, DarTar, Dark-Fire, Darkspy945, DarrenW, Darrenm540, David Edgar, David Woodward, Davidherman, Dawnseeker2000, Dbachmann, Dcxf, Deattitude, Degorr, Demysc, Denniss, Dennisthe2, Desbest, Dhaluza, Diamondland, Diannaa, Diblidabliduu, Diego Moya, Diego.viola, Digana, Digilee, Dingar, Dismas, Dj.cowan, Dlrohrer2003, Dmit, DmitryKo, Doeu, Dontmitchell, Douglaswth, Download, Dpupkov, Dra.vladvamp, Dragon 280, Drbreznjev, Dreaded Walrus, Drogonov, Drrll, Dsh13, Dsrivallabha, DudeThinking, Dudyk, Dueynz, Dvyjones, Dziedrius, E258, E2eamon, EEMIV, ESkog, Eaefremov, Eagle-slayor, Eapache, Ebe123, Echeese, Ecicpeeie, Ed Burnette, Ed Poor, EdBever, Edinburgh Wanderer, Edoe, Edward, Ej159, Ekerazha, Electron9, Elektron, Eleman, Elronxenu, Emurphy42, EngineerFromVega, Enigmaticland, Ennustaja, EonOmega, Erc, Eric 324, ErkinBatu, Esebi95, Esperius, Essayemyoung4009, Estemi, Ettrig, EugeneKay, Eugrus, Exien, Explorer25, Faddykeyboard, Fanatic.manav, Fangfufu, Fastily, FatalError, Fattmann, Fbtjock, Feedmecereal, Ferengi, Ffinder, Filmore, Finalius, Firefoxian, Fish and karate, Flatterworld, Flemmra, FileGeiFaUstMe262, Flinth, Flohack, Fluffylouis, Found5dollar, Fox hyx, Fran McCrory, Frap, FredTubale, Freddicus, Free French, Friginator, Frood, Fryn, Fsamuels, Furrykef, Fxhomie, Gabriel A. Zorrilla, Gainesk, Gaius Cornelius, Galaxytab, Gallagher783, Gary King, Gautamkishore, Gboxdance, Gchangetok, Gdm, Geary, Gegorg, Gerhman, Gh5046, Ghepeu, Ghettoblaster, Ghost650, Glany222, GlasGhost, GlassCobra, Glen 3B, Goa103, Gogo Dodo, Gogoloid, GoingBatty, Gokberks, GoldKanga, Golftheman, Good Olfactory, Googlemobileplatform, Googlesubculture, Gordon Ecker, GorillaWarfare, Gouranga Gupta, GraemeL, Grafen, Graft, Graig123, Grandscribe, GreenpeaceUbuntuMan, Gregconquest, Gregory Heffley, Gronky, Gsarwa, Gscshoyru, Gsonnenf, Gu1dry, Gudeldar, Gugu2903, Guitarguy99081, Gurch, Guru4321, Guyjohnston, Guzzyron, Gyro Copter, H4lfN3ls0n, HJ Mitchell, Haakon, Hacheema, Haggisfarm, Hammersoft, Hanifbbz, HardCorwen, Harizotoh9, Harp, Hcaandersen, Headinthedoor, Hedge777, Henriok, Henry W. Schmitt, Herakleitoszefesu, Hervegirod, Hgb asicwizard, Hockeyc, Hominid, Hoss789, HotXRock, Hotcrocodile, Howlingmadhowie, Htchien, Htinlinn90, Hu12, Hucz, Hughcharlesparker, Huku-chan, Hutchinsonam, Hydrox, Hymek, I Feel Tired, I, Podius, I5bala, IBoy2G, IGEL, IRWolfie-, ISTB351, Ian1337, IceHunter, Icep, Icydesign, Iggymwangi, Ijon, Iknowyourider, IlPisano, Illegal Operation, Imagine Reason, Immunmotbluescreen, Imroy, Indianstar, InternetMeme, Invenio, InverseHypercube, InvertedPendulum, Ionistii, Iridescent, Irishguy, Irislia, Ironmagma, Isaacwaller, Island Monkey, Iuhkjhk87y678, Ivant, Ivario, J.delanoy, JAMJAM1666, JEN9841, JHunterJ, JLMCGE01, Jack007, Jacob Poon, JacobSheehy, Jacobmathias, Jadden14, Jairodz, Jaizovic, Jamadagni, James Foster, JamesBWatson, JamesNBarnes, Jamgraham88, Jamougha, JaredMT, Jasper Deng, Javachan, JavierCane, JavierMC, Jb0807, Jboyens, Jbreckenridge, Jcogbil, Jdthood, JeR, Jeff G., Jeffq, Jeffrey Sharkey, Jeffwang, Jenova20, Jerebin, Jeromeds99, Jerrinsg, Jerryobject, Jesant13, Jessica23, Jhonnyx1000, Jiess, Jim1138, Jimmin, Jimthing, Jimv1983, Jinmyo, Jmcdon10, Jmecimore, JobiWan144, Joconnor, Joemalt1832, Johantheghost, John Ericson, JohnSawyer, Johnconorryan, Johndburger, Jokonek, Jonabbey, Jonathan-Morris711, JonathonSimister, Jonkerz, Jontintinjordan, Jopo, Jorge Stolfi, Joriki, JosJuice, Josh.e.stroud, JoshDuffMan, Jpvinall, Jreferee, Jrishel, Jtangsw, Jtfcobra, Jubeidono, Julesd, Jurisnipper, Jusses2, Jvosika, Jwkilgore, KAMiKAZOW, KDesk, Kaicarver, Kaisersushi, Karam.Anthony.K, Karthickmad, Katherine, Katoh, Kawasakik, KayoWikiP069, Kenny Strawn, Kentyman, Kevin James Field, Kevthegreat55, Kforeman1, Khalid hassani, Khanayub1986, Khr0n0s, Kiddington, Kien64, KimDabelsteinPetersen, Kingdowney, Kingpin13, Kinkate18nic, Kiore, Kitsunegami, Kkm010, Klemen Kocjancic, Klingoncowboy4, Kmdowns, Knud Winckelmann, Koavf, Kokken Tor, Koman90, Komitsuki, Kontar, Korkut00, Korkut000, Kozuch, Kraftlos, Krazywrath, Krc1185, Kris cs1, Kronox android, Ksyrie, Kungming2, Kushal one, Kylelnny, Kylesamani, LSUniverse, LafinJack, LancerEvolution ;, Lanilsson, Larrymcp, LarsHolmberg, LarsPensjo, Lbstone27, Legoboy920, Lenar, Lesmin, Lester, Lethe, Leuko, Levineps, Lexischemen, Lfcohen, Libcub, LightSpeed3, Lightenoughtotravel, Lightmouse, Lindamilton, Lindberg, Lkt1126, Llancast, Llewelyn MT, Logan, Logical Cowboy, Lokpest, LookingGlass, Lopifalko, LorenzoB, Lotje, Lovetinkle, Lucas.Yamanishi, Luckerr, Lun Esex, M0sia1, MER-C, MZMcBride, Mac, Macungie, Magioladitis, Mahanga, Male1979, Manop, Mantrik00, Mappum, Marc Lacoste, Marcus Brute, Marcus Qwertyus, Marcus2020, Mardus, Marek69, Mark Renier, Mark0528, Markmcwiggins, Marko Gargenta, Markpb91, Marksbark, Marqueed, Martin.komunide.com, Mastrsushi, Materialscientist, Mathewsherdil, Matt Darby, Matthew0028, MatthewBurton, MattieTK, Mattkap, Mattkap2, Maulikdave05, Maurice Carbonaro, Mauripop, Maxdeutc, Maximus06, Maxí, McGeddon, Mcld, Mdikici, Meepzip, Meersmaj, Melab-1, Melmann, Mendaliv, Mentifisto, Mephistophelian, Messiisking, MetaManFromTomorrow, Mewtu, Mharen, Michaelplourde66, Midgetman433, Mikael Häggström, Mike Rosoft, Mike.lifeguard, Milan Keršláger, Mild Bill Hiccup, Millstream3, Miltonhowe, Mimihitam, Mindmatrix, Minterior, Mirabilos, Miserlou, Mistral Mktg, Mistral Solutions, Mkouklis, Mobilepush, Modamoda, Mohanpram, Moneytoo, Moocha, Mordka, MoreNet, MoreThings, Mortense, Mr. Met 13, MrGALL, MrOllie, Ms2ger, Muelaner, Mugsywwiii, Mugunth Kumar, Mutchy126, MyNameWasTaken, Myas012, Myscrnnm, N2e, N5iln, NYKevin, Naddy, Nagy Dániel, Nagytam, Nahado, Namures, Nantasatria, Nathanloop, NeMeSiS, Nealmcb, NeilN, Neinsun, NetHunter, Newsoxy, NexuSix, Nexus26, Nicholas Love, Nick Garvey, Nico357, Nightscream, NiklasBr, Nikpapag, Ninly, Njonji, Nodekeeper, Nogburt, Noloader, Noozgroop, Norm mit, Now wiki, Nuclearmoose, Nuujinn, Nyco, Ofennell, Ohaaron, Ohnoitsjamie, OlavN, Old Number7, Oldmokmok, Oleg Alexandrov, Oli Filth, Omshivaprakash, Orange Suede Sofa, Originalwana, OsamaK, OspreyPL, OwenBlacker, Oxwil, P.Shack, P2jones, PILZI, Papatenor, Pascal.Honore, Patrick, Paulmlieberman, Paulscrawl, Pdfpdf, Peter712, Peterkagey, Pgan002, Phalinshah, Phatom87, Philip Trueman, PhosphoricX, Phy1729, Piast93, PieterDeBruijn, Pinball22, Pinecar, Pjedicke, Pkkasu, Plankhead, PlantRunner, Plarem, Plop, Pluma, Pmod, Pmyteh, Pokstad, Pol098, PolarYukon, Pomegranate, Pooooooooo123, Potentials, Pr4733k, PriceChild, Prius 2, Privateboz, Procedure, ProfPolySci45, Prolog, Prosfilaes, Prototypecreative, Pryanni, Psantora, Pseudomonas, Pvanderlee, Pwnage97, Quarkgluonsoup, Quartermaster, Quebec99, Quoth, Qwyrxian, RScheiber, Raburton, Rachel263, Raghualluri, Rahil.kassamali, Rajanbalana, Rajeshsweb, Ral725, Ralfsmouse, RameshaLB, Ramonrabello, Random name, Randomname66, Rapjul, Rapomon, Ravipokemon, Raysonho, Rborghese, Rchandra, RcketScientist, Reaper Eternal, RedHillian, Redekopmark, Reebsauce, Reedy, RegenerateThis, RenniePet, Res2216firestar, Resplendent, Rich Farmbrough, Richard Arthur Norton (1958-), Richi, Richiekim, Riffic, Rigelt, Riki, Ringbang, RingtailedFox, Rjwilmsi, Rmanke, Robbrown, Robert Moyse, RobertMfromLI, Roberth Edberg, Roberto.larcher, Robferrer, Robzz, Rocboronat, RockMFR, Rockysmile11, Rod92p, Rodeosmurf, Roguegeek, Roif456, Ronnies1312, RotaryAce, RoyBoy, Royce, Rprpr, Rugops, Runtime, Rush2009, Ryan8374, RyanQuinlan, RzR, Rzęsor, S1lencing, SF007, Sachinchavan.in, Sagarwal1981, Saifuddinap, Sailsbystars, Sainath468, Salamurai, Salazasu, Salvio giuliano, SamJohnston, Samdman95, Samkass, Samuh, Sandstein, SarekOfVulcan, Sasank, Sayden, Sbmeirow, Scampy11, Sciencewatcher, Scientus, Scl98029, ScottyWZ, Seanjacksontc, Searchmaven, Secretlondon, SephirothXIIIX, Seven.cardwell, SeyedKevin, Sfm 7, Shachar, Shadez08, Shadowjams, ShakataGaNai, Shaolinx, SharkD, Shaswat Narendra, Shevett, SidP, Sierra1bravo, Sigma2488, Sijil cv, Silvio Marano, Simonrleung, Simple Bob, Sjl0523, Skier Dude, Skierpage, Skudo900630, Slakr, Slatedorg, Sleepy Sentry, Sligocki, Small.is.powerful, Smashville, Smitty, Smyth, Snakeskincowboy, SoWhy, Socialmaven1, Solinym, Solipsys, Solomon Douglas, Soma6, Some jerk on the Internet, Someguy1221, Spaghetti64, Speculatrix, Spiel, Sreyan, Sriram sh, Staka, StaticGull, Steel, Stefan, Stephenb, Stephenwanjau, Steve03Mills, Steve1428, Stevedel7, Steveklein, Steven Walling, Stevenbz9, Stevenmitchell, Stevenwagner, StewieK, Strcat, Subbu, Suckystraw, Suction Man, SudoGhost, Sukael, Sunnypsyop, Sunray, Suzals3, SvGeloven, Svetovid, Svick, Swampyank, Sygmoral, Sylvainchevalierfu, Syndicate, Syp, T-Rex84, TMO KOTOR, TXI59, Tagrb03f, Tahitiville, Taras, TarzanJr, TastyCakes, Tavilis, Tbhotch, Tbird20d, Tcncv, Tedder, Tedickey, Teeks99, Teleprinter Sleuth, Teles, Tgeairn, The Anome, The Letter J, The359, TheEditrix2, TheTechFan, TheWishy, Thealexweb, Theanphibian, Theartfullodger, Thecurran91, Themfromspace, Thesamami, Thingg, ThomasWilson2, Thorwald, Thumperward, Thunder Wolf, Thunderbird8, Thüringer, Tide rolls, Timeshifter, TimmmmCam, Timneu22, TobiasPersson, Tobziez, Tomchen1989, Tomlzz1, Tomself1, Tondi5, Tony Sidaway, TonyW, TorQue Astur, Torqueing, Traal, Tracer9999, TrbleClef, Trebek Skates, Trefork, Tri400, Troed, Trusilver, Tsriopensourceblueprints, Tuxcantfly, Tweisbach, Txaggiemichael, U5K0, UKER, UU, Uirauna, Ujimatcha, Ulric1313, Unamed102, Unknownwarrior33, Urashimataro, Urfavoritemija, User931, Usmanahmed25, Vadmium, Van helsing, Varlaam, Vcelloho, Venona, Victorpardosi, Vincenzo.romano, Voidvector, VoluntarySlave, Vrenator, Vujke, WakiMiko, Walter Görlitz, Walterlmitchell3, Waltonkbbl, Watchcars, Wbison3, Wednesday Next, Wello95, Werbej, Werdna, Wertydm, Wesleyarchbell, WhatMeWork, Whatiknow, Wickedjacob, Wifuk, WikiLaurent, Wikigod, Wikipedian2009, Wild mine, William Leadford, Williameis, Windofkeltia, Wintermute115, Wizardist, Wknight94, Wlindley, Woohookitty, Woolfy123, Writermonique, Wtmitchell, Wwoods, XJamRastafire, Xavierorr, Xcrivener, XdaLive, Xhienne, Xiutwel-0003, Xnamkcor, Xomm, Xrobau, Xsspider, Xx3nvyxx, Y2kcrazyjoker4, YICbaby, Yadavjpr, Yahia.barie, Yamla, Yaohong3914, YasharF, Yellowdesk, Yiosie2356, Yngvarr, Yousou, Yug, Yuriybrisk, ZacBowling, ZamorakO o,

Žaratoustra, Zbutler7, Zeldex, Zero sharp, ZimZalaBim, Zipcodeman, ZirconiumTwice, Zorak950, Zouzzou, Zundark, Zunmun, Ammusaz, Ævar Arnfjörð Bjarmason, A, Սահակ, , , , 2399 anonymous edits

Tablet_computer *Source*: http://en.wikipedia.org/w/index.php?title=Tablet_computer *Contributors*: 842U, A Quest For Knowledge, AV3000, AakashTablet, Ace of Spades, AgadaUrbanit, Ahunt, Aizuku, Alefeb, Alisha.4m, Alvestrand, Ancheta Wis, Anders Feder, AndrewHowse, Andries, ArtsMusicFilm, BD2412, BKfi, Bender235, Bhny, Bidofthis, Bigredsky, Bikepunk2, Bob bobato, Camilo Sanchez, Captain-n00dle, Chrissb, Chuck369, Coercorash, CommonsDelinker, Crimsonmargarine, Crysb, Cvbommel, D.M. from Ukraine, DMY, DVdm, Daniel.Cardenas, Dawnseeker2000, Dbachmann, DenisRS, Dialectric, Diamondland, Diego Moya, Dondegroovily, Dougher, Drnick2, Edcolins, Editor2020, Edkollin, Elandy2009, Elizium23, Eog1916, Eraserhead1, ErkinBatu, Esebi95, EuTuga, Evan-Amos, EvertR25, Exlixe, Falcon9x5, Fieldafar, Fikri RA, Filing Flunky, Fishnet37222, Forresttsao, GSL-Nathan, Glenn, GreenZeb, Gsarwa, Hakimio, Heavyrain2408, Helmuthva, HiddenIP, Hydriz, Ionutpopa, Ipadtablet, Itsmine, IvanLanin, J.delanoy, JaGa, Javabyte, Jeffnailen, Jerryobject, Jgera5, Jim.henderson, Jinnai, JohnSawyer, JonathanDP81, Joy, Jpod2009, KKoolstra, Karlson2k, Karlww, Ketil, Kevdave, Krauss, Kyng, Leofranco2000, Lexischemen, LilHelpa, Lore1996, Lppa, Lun Esex, MER-C, Macromediax, Mahjongg, Marcos, Marcus Qwertyus, Materialscientist, Mcapdevila, Mckinley99, Merbabu, MetaManFromTomorrow, Michael Minh, Mikitei, Mr Stephen, Nateclev, Nesvarbu02, New Thought, Newone, Nijusby, Noozgroop, Ohconfucius, OlavN, OspreyPL, Pacey2007, PeregrineAY, Piotrus, Pnm, Proskillr, Red Act, Ric36, Ricvelozo, Ronz, Rostz, SF007, SamJohnston, Samarth.karwal, SarekOfVulcan, Sbmeirow, ScottSteiner, Scottywong, Shahimbaker, Shrish, Simonrleung, Socialmaven1, Soundvisions1, SpareHeadOne, Squids and Chips, Stimpy, Suso, Swarm, Szente, TMV943, Taka76, Tankwan, Taxman, Tgeairn, The Pikachu Who Dared, The Thing That Should Not Be, Tide rolls, Tomasohara, Tony Sidaway, Toussaint, Transmanche, Trevj, UCDS, Vanuan, Vrenator, Vyx, WOSlinker, Wbrito, Weylin.piegorsch, Wiki13, WilliamBrain, Woohookitty, WorldBrains, XJamRastafire, Xcvista, Yamaan, Yosh3000, Zc456, Ö1mageri, 210 anonymous edits

Android_Market *Source*: http://en.wikipedia.org/w/index.php?title=Android_Market *Contributors*: 20chances, 573W1E, 90 Auto, A bit iffy, Akbarzpro, Alex, Amaccuish, Amer-aln7l, Amlz, Amstuzmarco, Anderssl, Andrejavus, Aravindan Shanmugasundaram, Archee2, Artemisthemp, Barek, Beanlovin2, Belovedfreak, Benjaminohio, Bernie74, Bkonrad, Brianreading, Brilldoctor, Camos95, CaribDigita, CiaranG, CommonsDelinker, Coolaaron88, Crownmethod, Ctrl alt delboot, Curtisjones12345, Dale Arnett, Damian Yerrick, Davejohnsan, Dcxf, Duncan, Efalk, Ekhcsub, Elonka, Etbal, Falcon8765, Frap, FreewareLovers, Frmorrison, Furrykef, Fyxim, Gary King, George.chri, Giraffedata, GoingBatty, Googlepapi, Griffin5, Gsarwa, HHeimbuerger, HOueLin4, Haha01haha01, Hammsidh, Hanifbbz, Hedge777, Hervegirod, Hoss789, Huaiwei, Iadrian yu, Ieee8023, Ilickedyomomma, JJC1138, JLaTondre, James Foster, Jamietw, Jan Winnicki, JavierCane, Jayaramanettar, Jdthood, Jeffq, Jenskristian, Jerryobject, Jim1138, JimmyBanks6, Joeattardi, John Lucas, JohnDoe0007, Jorrro, Joy, KDesk, Kencf0618, Kenny Strawn, Kenosando, Kitallisiki, Kokken Tor, Kolipon, Kontar, Krupagj, Lamarguy91, Leedsunited92, Legoboy920, Lester, Libcub, Lindberg, MER-C, Maarschalk, MagentaCyan, Mahahahaneapneap, Mairi, Mark0528, Mattkap2, McGeddon, Mdikici, Mdwh, Messiisking, Mgfawzi, Mike.lifeguard, Milominderbinder2, Moneytoo, Murthag06, Nahado, Nezdek, Ohconfucius, Omart, Peak, Pgagge, Philipdaubmeier, Planetary Chaos Redux, Pnm, Poolback, PutzfetzenORG, Pyfan, Queen of Awesome, Quoth, Qwayzer, R'n'B, Rahil.kassamali, Ral725, Reebsauce, Revaaron, Rockysmile11, Rowdy1974, Rowilpe, Rzęsor, SF007, SQL, SchmuckyTheCat, Secator, Senikk, Sidduz, Skandalfo, Slideme, Smsarmad, Smstextmobile, Soewinhan, Solsticedhiver, Spurlos89, Sross (Public Policy), Steel, Stranger Dan, Stromcarlson, SudoGhost, Sven1703, Sylviarenee, Themfromspace, Thumperward, Timing, Tnxman307, TomXP411, Tomself1, Tonkie67, Trevj, Truthanado, Uncle Dick, Velella, Vicky Ng, Vinu76jsr, WPSamson, Wazerrr, Woolfy123, Wwahammy, Yworo, Zesel, Zouzzou, Zquinn3, 397 anonymous edits

Random-access_memory *Source*: http://en.wikipedia.org/w/index.php?title=Random-access_memory *Contributors*: 0612, 128mem, 1exec1, 28421u2232nfenfcenc, 28bytes, 2TerabyteBox =Josh.Harris, ALEF7, AThing, Aapo Laitinen, Abjm, Accurizer, Addera, Adlen, AdultSwim, Aitias, Akuyume, Akyoyo94, Alan1000, Alansohn, Ale jrb, AlefZet, AlexanderDS, Alfio, Ali@gwc.org.uk, Alucard sigma, Amaurea, AnMaster, Anagy22, Anaxial, Andonic, Andrejj, Andres, Andrewy, Andy M. Wang, Andyjsmith, Andypandy.UK, Angelic Wraith, Anikingos, Ansible, Antandrus, AnthonyA7, Antman, Anuragiscool12, Aogus, Arbraini, Arkrishna, ArnoldReinhold, Arvindn, Asanchez1572, Asapilu, Aschmitz, Aslihanbilgekurt, Atulsnischal, Austinmurphy, Ayecee, B0at, BR01097, BW52, Bachrach44, Balderdash707, Barticus88, Basak327, Bawolff, Bdamokos, Bdskene, Beland, Ben D., Ben-Zin, Bencherlite, Benjeeeboy, Benjiboi, Berkut, BernardH, Beyond silence, Bjf, Blackdogman, Blanchardb, Blinklad, Bloigen, Bmonro, Bmunden, Bob360bob360, Bobagoncheese, Bobanater, Bobblewik, Bobo192, Bonadea, Bongwarrior, Boothy443, BorgHunter, Boulaur, Bped1985, Brianga, Brianski, Brion VIBBER, Brookie, Brother Dysk, Bruce1ee, Bsdjkqvfkj, Burntsauce, Bwhack, CASIO F-91W, CAkira, Cahk, Calamari, Caltas, Camboxer, Camerong, Can't sleep, clown will eat me, CanisRufus, Capricorn42, Catgut, Cbuckley, Cctoombs, Cessator, Chaheel Riens, Charleca, Charlieleake, Cheesechords, ChipChamp, Christian List, CiaPan, Ciphers, CityOfSilver, Ckape, Clueless newbie, CoJaBo, CodeMaster123, Coercorash, ComputerWizerd, Conversion script, Cool110110, Coremayo, Corixidae, Corpx, Craggyisland, Crakkpot, Crispmuncher, Critikal, Crusadeonilliteracy, Crzysdrs, Cst17, Ctech72, Czarkoff, DARTH SIDIOUS 2, DMacks, DVD R W, DVdm, Damian Yerrick, Dancter, Daranz, Darth Panda, DarylNickerson, DavidCary, DavidH, Davodd, Dchidest, Deathanatos, Deking305, DerHexer, DexDor, Dharmuone, Diannaa, Dimo414, DirkvdM, Discospinster, Djbdan, Doanjackson, DocWatson42, DocendoDiscimus, Dosman, Douglas Whitaker, Download, Drhex, Drrngrvy, Dustimagic, Dzubint, Długosz, ELCleanup, ERcheck, Edderso, Editor911, Edward321, Eehite, Eggman183, Egmontaz, ElfWarrior, Elvir.doc, Emx, Enchanter, Enviroboy, Epbr123, Eric-Wester, EvanSeeds, Excirial, Explicit, Falcon8765, Favonian, Fervidfrogger, Fillepa, Fireaxe888, Firetrap9254, Flewis, Flowerpotman, Fnagaton, Frap, Frappucino, Frecklefoot, Frieda, Frosty3219, Funkyj, Fyrael, Fyyer, GCFreak2, Gadfium, Gaius Cornelius, Gamer007, Gapaddict, Gareth Aus, Geljamin, Geniac, Giftlite, Gjeremy, Glass Sword, Glenn, Gogo Dodo, Gonzo fan2007, GoodDamon, Goodnightmush, Gopherbob1921, Gordeonbleu, Gracefool, Graham87, Greg847, Gregbard, Grendwx, Grinters, Grstain, Guardianangelz, Gurch, Guthrie, Guy Harris, Hadal, Halcionne, HalfShadow, Halmstad, Hariraja, Harp, Hazel77, Hbent, Heaviestcat, HeirloomGardener, HenkeB, Heron, Hikmet483, Hirohisat, Hllomen, Hobartimus, Holizz, Hoo man, Hsn6161, Hughey, Hughtcool, Hulleye, Husond, Huw Powell, Hwan051, Hydrogen Iodide, ICE77, Il MusLiM HyBRiD II, IRP, Iced-T, Icelight, Igoldste, Ikebowen, Imran, Inaneframe, Infernowolf36, Insanity Incarnate, Irbisgreif, IronGargoyle, Ironicart, Irwangatot, Island, Isnow, Itsacon, Iulianu, Ixfd64, J.delanoy, J00tel, J04n, JForget, JaGa, Jaakobou, Jab843, James Anthony Knight, James084, Jascii, Jasper Deng, Jasz, JayC, Jbolden1517, JeLuF, Jeff G., Jeffrey O. Gustafson, Jennavecia, Jerome Charles Potts, Jerry1964, Jesse Viviano, Jfmantis, Jgreenberg, Jheald, Jic, Jimfile, Jimothytrotter, Jni, JoanneB, Joeblakesley, John Millikin, John.jml739, John254, JonHarder, Jonhjelm, Jonomacdrones, JoshuaZ, Jsharpminor, Juckum, Judy74, Julz888, K. Annoyomous, KB Alpha, KD5TVI, Kagemaru16, KaiKemmann, Kain Nihil, Kannmaeh, Karmic, Keilana, Keithonearth, Kelly Martin, Kelvingeorge, KennethJ, Kesac, Kevin chen2003, Khanbm, Kickkmyfaceinn, KieferSkunk, King Arthur6687, Kingpin13, Kjkolb, Kman543210, KnowledgeOfSelf, Kozuch, Krich, Kubanczyk, L Kensington, LOL, LSD, LX, Lando Calrissian, LarsHolmberg, Law, LeaveSleaves, LedgendGamer, LeoNomis, Lerdsuwa, Leslie Mateus, Licensedlunacy, Lilac Soul, Lipatden, LizardJr8, Llakais, Logicwiki, Looper5920, Lotu, Lova Falk, Lovok, Lpetrazickis, Luk, Lukep913, Luna Santin, Lupacchione, MER-C, Mac, Madhero88, Majorly, Malafaya, Mani1, Manlyspidersporkadmin, Mart22n, Martin451, Masamage, Maschelos, Masterofabcs, MateoCorazon, Materialscientist, Matma Rex, Matt Britt, Mattimeeleo, Maury Markowitz, Mav, Maxxdxx, Mayumashu, Mbessey, Mboverload, Mdkoch84, Mechanical digger, Med, Megaman en m, Melsaran, Mentifisto, Mhnin0, Mike Dill, Mike Rosoft, Mild Bill Hiccup, Mindloss, MindyTan, Mindymoo22, Miquonranger03, Mirage-project, Mistercow, Monkey Bounce, Moogle001, Moreati, MorganaFiolett, MorrisRob, Mouse Nightshirt, Moxfyre, MrFish, MrOllie, Mulad, Mulder416, Mulligan's Wake, Muugokszhiion, Myanw, Mygerardromance, Myke2020, NYKevin, Nakon, NawlinWiki, Ned Scott, Nepenthes, Newport Beach, NicAgent, Nintnt, Nixeagle, Njardarlogar, Nmacu, Nmagedman, Noah Salzman, Norm, Notting Hill in London, Nsaa, Nyvhek, Obradovic Goran, Ochib, Odie5533, Oicumayberight, Oiketohn, Oliverdl, OlofE, Omicronpersei8, Ommel, Onur074, Optimist on the run, Orannis, OrbitOne, Oroso, Orphic, Owain, Oxydo, Oxymoron83, Papercutbiology, Parnell88, Pboyd, Pcb21, Pcb95, Pcj, Pearle, Pedro, Persian Poet Gal, Peruvianllama, Peter.C, Peterl, Peyre, Pgan002, Pgk, PhilKnight, Philip Trueman, PhilipO, Pnnguyen, Possum, Prakashkumaraman, Profgadd, Proofreader77, Puchiko, Purpledramallama, Qatter, Qwyrxian, Qxz, R. S. Shaw, RJaguar3, Radon210, RainbowOfLight, Ramu50, Raven4x4x, Ravenperch, RazielZero, Razorflame, Real NC, Reconsider the static, Reddysan345, Res2216firestar, RexNL, Rhobite, Rich Farmbrough, Richard D. LeCour, Ricky81682, Ridge Runner, Riferimento, Rilak, Ripepette, Rj, Roadrunner, Robert K S, Robert Merkel, Robertvan1, Roguecomgeek, Rollie, Rossumcapek, RoyBoy, Rrburke, Ryan8bit, SDJ, SJP, SWAdair, Sagaciousuk, Sagark86, Samuelim24, Sarenne, Sat84, Savannah Kaylee, Scarian, Scarypeep, SciberDoc, Scott14, Seahorseruler, Seesh cabeesh, Seksek, SeoMac, Sfoskett, Shadow demon, Shadowlynk, Shandris, Shanes, Shawnhath, Shaz929, SheeEttin, Shinji008, Shoeofdeath, Shreshth91, Shubham18, Sigma 7, Sillydragon, Sinohayja, Sjö, Skeddles, SkyWalker, Slakr, Slowking Man, Snydale, Sol Blue, Solidsnake204, Some jerk on the Internet, Souvik100, Sparkiegeek, Spike Wilbury, SpuriousQ, Ssd, Steevm, Stephen, Stephen Gilbert, Stevertigo, Stevethepanda, Stickee, Stryn, Suffusion of Yellow, Super IT guy, Synchrite, THEN WHO WAS PHONE?, THF, TVX109, TaintedZebra, Tangotango, Tawker, Tealwisp, Techdawg667, Tehh bakery, The Anome, The Cunctator, The Interior, The Rambling Man, The Thing That Should Not Be, The undertow, TheDoober, TheJosh, TheLurkerMan, Theamazingswamp, Theqwert, Thingg, Think outside the box, ThinkBlue, Thisisborin9, Thorpe, Thumperward, Tide rolls, Timmahlicious, Timmy mctimmy, Tintii, Toddst1, TomPhil, Tony Sidaway, Traroth, Trevor MacInnis, Tridian, Triona, Tubby23, Tvdinnerkid, Twilight1188, Typhlosion, Uncle Dick, Uncle G, UncleBubba, Urhixidur, Usb10, Useight, VampWillow, Vanished895703, Vcolin, Velella, Versus22, Vilerage, ViriiK, Vishnava, Vivio Testarossa, Voyagerfan5761, Vsmith, Wafulz, Weregerbil, Wernher, Wesley, West.andrew.g, Whkoh, WikiSlasher, Wikiloop, Wikipelli, William Avery, Wimt, Wizardist, Wizzy, WookieInHeat, Work permit, Worthlessboy1420, Wowkiddymage, Wtshymanski, Xionbox, Xpclient, YUL89YYZ, Yansa, Yekrats, Yidisheryid, Yogiz, Yunshui, Yurik, Yyy, ZS, ZX81, Zachlipton, Zara1709, Zero sharp, ZeroOne, Zhile, Zhou Yu, Zim Lex, Zita127, Zondor, ملاع بوبحم, 1821 anonymous edits

DataWind *Source*: http://en.wikipedia.org/w/index.php?title=DataWind *Contributors*: 842U, Abdul raja, Afaber012, BD2412, Ben Ben, Jpmeena, Kkm010, Mandarax, Marrante, Pnm, Woohookitty, 5 anonymous edits

GetJar *Source*: http://en.wikipedia.org/w/index.php?title=GetJar *Contributors*: Blanchardb, Dawynn, Egil, Frmorrison, Gytaz, Ianis G. Vasilev, Jimbo Wales, JohnCD, Lawren00, Mathiastck, Netgarden, Pnm, R'n'B, Rzv, SF007, Sauls, 10 anonymous edits

NDTV *Source*: http://en.wikipedia.org/w/index.php?title=NDTV *Contributors*: AMuraliKumar, Abhi2point0, Abhishekg.a, Aec is away, Aerosumeet, Ageo020, Agrawal.ayush, Ajayprasad7, Akvenkat, Anbuphy, Anishniranam, Anshuk, Anupchak, Aprasannakumar, Arun.arumugam, Aryan wiki, Auric, Avik pram, Awesomdude123, AxG, Binand, Binglejoy, Bjoshi.in, Bobo192, Capricorn42, Cesar.medic, Ceyockey, Chanvis18, Chetanbatts, Chirag, Cloudcounts, CommonsDelinker, Crackjack, DARTH SIDIOUS 2, DMacks, DaGizza, Destiny121314, Divyanshuduttaroy, Dv82matt, Editor3008, Eelamstylez77, Ekabhishek, El C, Emarsee, Enigmaticanant, Fieldday-sunday, Forhiddenfacts, Galoiserdos, Gazzathebad, Giftiger wunsch, Gnusbiz, Gokulchandola, Gorgeousgia, GorillaWarfare, Greaterbabloo, Havak, Hibernian, Iam4Lost, Icecoolsushobhan, Ironholds, Ixfd64, JPMcGrath, Jasmeet 181, Jay.littlewing, Jezhotwells, Joshdboz, Jovianeye, Kaiba, Kaifazam, Kbdank71, Khan Afzal, Killiondude, Kindeditor, Kkm010, Krishnaprasaths, Krypton wolf, LICENSETOKILL, Laxstar1, Laxstar5, Lazypost, Libertyprevails, Lutherburbank, MakeRocketGoNow, Manjari.Chowdhury, Marek69, Marianian, Marshall1984, Martial75, Mauls, MikeDogma, Mikeo, Mmace91, Mrschimpf, Nabablucknow, Ndtvnasdaq, Newageindian, Nirvana888, Onco p53, Pacchu77, Paralympic, Philip Trueman, Pieguy48, PigFlu Oink, Porqin, Pradeepsomani, Prasa1, Pratyush Chowdhary, Primequbit, Psmith fan, RL0919, Rajeshroshan, Rjwilmsi, Rohit7dhiman, Roux-HG, SarekOfVulcan, Seb az86556, Selva20, Shanata, Sharikc, Sir Nicholas de Mimsy-Porpington, Stochos, Stuartfanning, Surelyhappy, T rsengup, T-rex, TheRealFennShysa, Themarcuscreature, Tinucherian, Tri400, Trickytext, UnitedStatesian, Utcursch, Vijayarumugam, Vinod m99, WhisperToMe, Xmpcray, Xyn1, Yogithebest, Žiedas, 356 anonymous edits

Subscriber_identity_module *Source*: http://en.wikipedia.org/w/index.php?title=Subscriber_identity_module *Contributors*: 001.keshav, 16@r, A3RO, A5b, Abdull, Aido2002, Ale jrb, Aled D, Alex.tan, Alexburke, Amicaveritas, Andrewferrier, Andros 1337, Anthony Ivanoff, Arnel enero, Asdino, Ashkhan, Ashwin, Askari Mark, Audin, Audriusa, AxG, Bahram.zahir, Baloo rch, Bart.vanassche, Bencherlite, BigHairRef, Bogybogy, Bombay01, Bouvierjr, Bratch, Brighterorange, Bsoft, Bubbachuck, Bwpach, C Ruth, Cap'n Refsmmat, CaribDigita, Chrislk02, ChuckBiggs2, Ckatz, Clawed, ClementSeveillac, CommonsDelinker, DBlomgren, DWaterson, Dabombazzz, Daemondust, Dale Arnett, Daniel.o.jenkins, Danno uk, Darac, David Traynor, DavidRCrowe, DerHexer, Dirkbb, Dkastner, DmitTrix, Dmitrytorba, DocWatson42, Dodger, Dreadstar, Dtedthingy, Dtobias, Duckbill, Duncan, Ed g2s, Edin1, Egil, Electron9, Elv2003, EnTheMohammad, Etmjang, Excirial, Fangfufu, Foofy, Foosterhoff, Frap, Gadfium, Gamelore, Gary King, Geoff Plourde, Georgy90, Ghettoblaster, Glane23, Gorm, Gr8dude, Grafen, Griffin5, Guinness2702, Guy Harris, Hadal, Hanche, Helpfulweasal, Heron, Hmwith, Hu12, Hutchyy, Hydrargyrum, Iced Kola, Improv, Isnow, JLD, Jarijokela, Jbroderi, Jcarella, Jdulaney, Jeff Song, Jeffq, Jerome Charles Potts, Jerryobject, Jimmayoy007, John of Reading, Johnsonja, Johnuniq, Jojalozzo, Jonathan Oldenbuck, Josemanimala, Jpatokal, Jtjdt, Julesd, Julien, Julo, Justin Ormont, Karl.brown, Katieh5584, KeithTyler, KelleyCook, Kiran Gopi, KnightRider, Koman90, Kostpolt, Krymson, L33th4x0rguy, Leion, LtNOWIS, Luna Santin, MARKELLOS, MaGa, Mac, Mackeriv, Martarius, MartynDavies, Mauls, MaxiLego, Meleegy, Metageek, Metagraph, Michael Hardy, Mik01aj, MikeKn, Mintleaf, Mitch Ames, Mmsarfraz, Modster, Mojodaddy, Moocha, Moocowsrock, Moraja, Mr Minchin, Mroach, Mushroom, Nanda, Nathan Hamblen, Neelix, Nelhage, NerdyNSK, Nikevich, Nil Einne, NiteowlneiIs, Nivix, Nokezie, ObuK, Ocram, Ohnoitsjamie, Olivier, Omegatron, Oosoom, Panindra, Pascal.Tesson, Paul August, Paul Marshall UK, Pc123-123, Peter Karlsen, Petertorr, Phantomsteve, Plaws, Plustgarten, Pnm, Ponydepression, Pushp vashisht, Pythoulon, Qxz, Radagast83, RadioActive, Raindeer, Rairden, Ravedave, Rjwilmsi, Romanskolduns, Ronhjones, Rossumcapek, Rubena, Salimfadhley, Sanders muc, Satori Son, Scepia, Sega381, Shadowjams, Shaimay2, Shan2097, Shirishag75, Shubhrajyoti.ece, Sidasta, SilentForce, Silverxxx, Simon Shek, Simonjwall, Sin Harvest, Situwei, Skeejay, Slakr, Sligocki, Slusk, Smalljim, Smyth, Snuffkin, Spa34a, Squash, Starshadow, Stephan Leeds, SteveSims, SudoGhost, Suicidalhamster, SuperMog2002, SystemBuilder, T0ky0, TBadger, Taka76, Talrias, Tapuwiki, Tentoila, Teque5, The Thing That Should Not Be, TheFallenCrowd, Thumperward, Timeastor, TitaniumDreads, Titoxd, Tngu77, Toh, Tom.k, TonyW, Toolnut, Tothwolf, Towel401, Trasz, Tripbeetle, Triwbe, UmbertoCorponi, UncleDouggie, Unixxx, Unyoyega, Utuado, Uzume, Vegaswikian, Velella, Vicentemf, Virgofenix, Watgap, Wfaulk, Whpq, Wideangle, Wikijimmy, Wikiklrsc, Wikiliki, Wingman358, Xompanthy, Xrtc, Yelyos, Yvh11a, ZIKRIE, ZXIII, Zaian, Zarcillo, Zephyris, Zeugma fr, Zr40, 427 anonymous edits

2G *Source*: http://en.wikipedia.org/w/index.php?title=2G *Contributors*: Acroterion, Alansohn, Andros 1337, Arda Xi, Baloo rch, BenFrantzDale, Bencey, Bobo192, Borgx, Bressen, Bshewmake, Chaldor, Cliff, Comediante, Conti, DVdm, Darrell Greenwood, Daveespionage, DavidWBrooks, Denisutku, Dlrohrer2003, Dremora, Eric, EwaDuan, Fang Aili, Frenchwhale, Fudoreaper, Gh5046, Glenn, Goofrider, Gscshoyru, Guy M, Hadiyana, HellDragon, Iandiver, InternetMeme, Jayden54, JohnTechnologist, Josep1c, Jpatokal, Jwrosenzweig, Ksn, LiDaobing, Lightmouse, Logan, LovesMacs, MMuzammils, Mafmafmaf, Malcolma, Mange01, Markalex, Maximus Rex, Mbehrns, MechMykl, Mgloerich, Mikaey, Mikemoral, Mlewis000, Mojodaddy, Muhandes, N0YKG, Nasa-verve, Naveenvrnew, Newone, Nisselua, Oknazevad, Otrfan, Pekaje, Phobie, Puffin, R'n'B, Radiojon, Redeagle688, Rettetast, Rjwilmsi, Smack, Snickerdo, Suffusion of Yellow, Tedder, Thingg, TigerShark, Tomi T Ahonen, Travidillo, TrevorBriggsCook, Utcursch, Vassyana, Vegaswikian, Vkgenjoy, Voidxor, Wayfarer, Wst, Wtmitchell, 118 anonymous edits

General_Packet_Radio_Service *Source*: http://en.wikipedia.org/w/index.php?title=General_Packet_Radio_Service *Contributors*: *drew, 24alpha, 4th guy, 63.192.137.xxx, A5b, ALM scientist, Abduljalil859, Abhinavvaid, Abldvlpr, Ahoerstemeier, Alastairgbrown, Ali@gwc.org.uk, AlistairMcMillan, Andrejj, Andros 1337, Andypdavis, Anetode, Angrytoast, Aninhumer, Antonski, Arvinarya, Astronautics, Badanedwa, Baloo rch, Banej, Barneca, Ben-Zin, Bering, Bhawani Gautam, Billylikeswikis, BirdbrainedPhoenix, Bobblewik, Cacophony, Capricorn42, Captain-n00dle, Carnildo, Carre, Charliearcuri, ChrisUK, Conti, Conversion script, Crashmatrix, Cryptext, Cygs 0007, DaedalusRaistlin, Dafocus, Davidisom, Dawnseeker2000, Dcarriso, Defeatedfear, Dennis Bratland, Depictionimage, DerHexer, Dgtsyb, Diannaa, DoubleBlue, Dr. Zaret, Dysprosia, EagleOne, EdoDodo, Edward, Email4mobile, EnTheMohammad, Engineerism, Ergosteur, Esnible, Europrobe, Euryalus, Evergreen9, EwaDuan, Extraordinary, FH 3, Flemimra, Frazzydee, Fuzheado, Gaius Cornelius, Gjivan, Gzkn, Hadal, Hadiyana, Hallje, HamburgerRadio, Hede2000, Hemanshu, Hgonzale, Hhan, Hohum, Hydrargyrum, IGeMiNix, INkubusse, Iandiver, Inter, Intgr, Inzy, Jackerhack, Jacooks, Jasonauk, Jemuel, Jim.henderson, Jklin, Jnavas, Jonathanriddell, Joseph Solis in Australia, KB1KOI, Karada, KingOfSofa, Kmbsww, Ksn, Learns visits aw, Lerdsuwa, Leszek Jańczuk, LeviathinXII, Liftarn, Lightmouse, LoopZilla, Luen, MC MasterChef, MER-C, Mac, Mange01, Manumg, Mathiastck, Maximus Rex, Mentifisto, Michael Hardy, Mike Rosoft, Mittosi, Mojodaddy, Monty Dickerson, Mozzerati, N0YKG, NPalmius, Nageh, Nakon, Neale Monks, Nil Einne, Nmnogueira, Novldp, Nwynder, Ohnoitsjamie, Oli Filth, Omegatron, One half 3544, Palopt, Pan Camel, Patrick, Pb30, Pbook8989, PeteVerdon, Pgan002, PhilHibbs, Piano non troppo, Plamka, Plasmaroo, Pmuschi, Pratyeka, Prolog, Qasdfdsaq, RHaworth, Radiojon, Rajeshnawal, Raohammad, Requestion, Rettetast, Rich257, Richardcraib, Ricky lais, Rjstott, Roberts83, Seancdaug, Seaphoto, Seikku Kaita, Sesu Prime, Shadowjams, Shahzad11, Shinpah1, Silvermane, Slashme, Smalljim, Smhanov, SpaceFlight89, Spel-Punc-Gram, Starszz, Stevehughes, Stinkinrich88, Stuart Ward UK, Sudeeprg, Svinodh, Swhitehead, Tex23, The Thing That Should Not Be, Thierry Bingen, Thue, Tom Morris, Tombomp, Tommike125, Tommy2010, Tooki, Trevor MacInnis, TutterMouse, Tyz, Utuado, Vegaswikian, Vipul, Vk2tds, Wapxana, Wik, WikiSysop2, Wikiliki, Winged-stone, Wo.luren, Woohookitty, Wrs1864, Wtmitchell, Youssefsan, Yury Tarasievich, Zzedar, Саша Стефановић, 488 anonymous edits

Image Sources, Licenses and Contributors

File:UbiSlate7.jpg *Source*: http://en.wikipedia.org/w/index.php?title=File:UbiSlate7.jpg *License*: unknown *Contributors*: Edited by Kesavan Muthuvel [k7.india]

Image:Indian Rupee symbol.svg *Source*: http://en.wikipedia.org/w/index.php?title=File:Indian_Rupee_symbol.svg *License*: unknown *Contributors*: User:Orionist

File:Android robot.svg *Source*: http://en.wikipedia.org/w/index.php?title=File:Android_robot.svg *License*: unknown *Contributors*: Google

File:Android logo.png *Source*: http://en.wikipedia.org/w/index.php?title=File:Android_logo.png *License*: unknown *Contributors*: Google

File:Android 4.0.png *Source*: http://en.wikipedia.org/w/index.php?title=File:Android_4.0.png *License*: unknown *Contributors*: Android Open Source project

File:System-architecture.jpg *Source*: http://en.wikipedia.org/w/index.php?title=File:System-architecture.jpg *License*: unknown *Contributors*: Jgaliana, MB-one

File:Android home.png *Source*: http://en.wikipedia.org/w/index.php?title=File:Android_home.png *License*: unknown *Contributors*: Unamed102

File:Galaxy Nexus smartphone.jpg *Source*: http://en.wikipedia.org/w/index.php?title=File:Galaxy_Nexus_smartphone.jpg *License*: unknown *Contributors*: Faramarz, MB-one, SF007, 1 anonymous edits

File:Google TV Screenshot.png *Source*: http://en.wikipedia.org/w/index.php?title=File:Google_TV_Screenshot.png *License*: unknown *Contributors*: Tokyoship

File:Androidmarket3311.png *Source*: http://en.wikipedia.org/w/index.php?title=File:Androidmarket3311.png *License*: unknown *Contributors*: Griffin5, SF007

File:AndroidMarketPermissions.png *Source*: http://en.wikipedia.org/w/index.php?title=File:AndroidMarketPermissions.png *License*: unknown *Contributors*: Amlz, SoWhy

File:Android chart.png *Source*: http://en.wikipedia.org/w/index.php?title=File:Android_chart.png *License*: unknown *Contributors*: Android Open Source project

File:IFA 2010 Internationale Funkausstellung Berlin 03.JPG *Source*: http://en.wikipedia.org/w/index.php?title=File:IFA_2010_Internationale_Funkausstellung_Berlin_03.JPG *License*: unknown *Contributors*: User:Bin im Garten

File:IFA 2010 Internationale Funkausstellung Berlin 18.JPG *Source*: http://en.wikipedia.org/w/index.php?title=File:IFA_2010_Internationale_Funkausstellung_Berlin_18.JPG *License*: unknown *Contributors*: User:Bin im Garten

File:-order.gif *Source*: http://en.wikipedia.org/w/index.php?title=File:-order.gif *License*: unknown *Contributors*: Aotake, Sarang, Swift, Wikic

File:-red.png *Source*: http://en.wikipedia.org/w/index.php?title=File:-red.png *License*: unknown *Contributors*: Sarang, Ymursal, Yug

File:Lenovo-X61-Tablet-Mode.jpg *Source*: http://en.wikipedia.org/w/index.php?title=File:Lenovo-X61-Tablet-Mode.jpg *License*: unknown *Contributors*: User:Evan-Amos

File:N800 frontside2.jpg *Source*: http://en.wikipedia.org/w/index.php?title=File:N800_frontside2.jpg *License*: unknown *Contributors*: Zxc

File:IPad in Case.jpg *Source*: http://en.wikipedia.org/w/index.php?title=File:IPad_in_Case.jpg *License*: unknown *Contributors*: Yutaka Tsutano

File:ASUS_Eeepad_Transformer_with_Dock_Keyboard.JPG *Source*: http://en.wikipedia.org/w/index.php?title=File:ASUS_Eeepad_Transformer_with_Dock_Keyboard.JPG *License*: unknown *Contributors*: User:Fieldafar

File:Xo3-fuse-2.jpg *Source*: http://en.wikipedia.org/w/index.php?title=File:Xo3-fuse-2.jpg *License*: unknown *Contributors*: laptop.org

File:Android Market.png *Source*: http://en.wikipedia.org/w/index.php?title=File:Android_Market.png *License*: unknown *Contributors*: Andrejavus, Salavat, Skier Dude, Zouzzou

File:Android Market website.png *Source*: http://en.wikipedia.org/w/index.php?title=File:Android_Market_website.png *License*: unknown *Contributors*: SF007, Sfan00 IMG, Skier Dude

File:Android Market.jpg *Source*: http://en.wikipedia.org/w/index.php?title=File:Android_Market.jpg *License*: unknown *Contributors*: User:PetarM

Image:Memory module DDRAM 20-03-2006.jpg *Source*: http://en.wikipedia.org/w/index.php?title=File:Memory_module_DDRAM_20-03-2006.jpg *License*: unknown *Contributors*: A.Savin, Afrank99, Cyberdex, H005, Qurren, Tothwolf, 8 anonymous edits

File:Bundesarchiv Bild 183-1989-0406-022, VEB Carl Zeiss Jena, 1-Megabit-Chip.jpg *Source*: http://en.wikipedia.org/w/index.php?title=File:Bundesarchiv_Bild_183-1989-0406-022,_VEB_Carl_Zeiss_Jena,_1-Megabit-Chip.jpg *License*: unknown *Contributors*: Kasper, Jan Peter

File:RamTypes.JPG *Source*: http://en.wikipedia.org/w/index.php?title=File:RamTypes.JPG *License*: unknown *Contributors*: User:KB Alpha

File:Datawind logo.png *Source*: http://en.wikipedia.org/w/index.php?title=File:Datawind_logo.png *License*: unknown *Contributors*: 842U, Danlaycock

File:GetJar_logo.jpg *Source*: http://en.wikipedia.org/w/index.php?title=File:GetJar_logo.jpg *License*: unknown *Contributors*: Egil

File:NDTV logo.svg *Source*: http://en.wikipedia.org/w/index.php?title=File:NDTV_logo.svg *License*: unknown *Contributors*: NDTV

file:SIM Card.jpg *Source*: http://en.wikipedia.org/w/index.php?title=File:SIM_Card.jpg *License*: unknown *Contributors*: User:Georgy90

file:SIM Card Holder.jpg *Source*: http://en.wikipedia.org/w/index.php?title=File:SIM_Card_Holder.jpg *License*: unknown *Contributors*: Richard Wheeler (Zephyris)

file:Tf sim both sides.png *Source*: http://en.wikipedia.org/w/index.php?title=File:Tf_sim_both_sides.png *License*: unknown *Contributors*: User:Koman90

file:SIM chip structure and packaging.svg *Source*: http://en.wikipedia.org/w/index.php?title=File:SIM_chip_structure_and_packaging.svg *License*: unknown *Contributors*: User:Justin Ormont

file:GSM Micro SIM Card vs. GSM Mini Sim Card.svg *Source*: http://en.wikipedia.org/w/index.php?title=File:GSM_Micro_SIM_Card_vs._GSM_Mini_Sim_Card.svg *License*: unknown *Contributors*: User:Justin Ormont

file:Telia micro SIM with brackets.jpg *Source*: http://en.wikipedia.org/w/index.php?title=File:Telia_micro_SIM_with_brackets.jpg *License*: unknown *Contributors*: User:Mroach

file:Disassembled SIM Card Film.JPG *Source*: http://en.wikipedia.org/w/index.php?title=File:Disassembled_SIM_Card_Film.JPG *License*: unknown *Contributors*: User:Dabombazzz

File:Embedded SIM from M2M supplier Eseye with an adapter board for evaluation in a Mini-SIM socket.jpg *Source*: http://en.wikipedia.org/w/index.php?title=File:Embedded_SIM_from_M2M_supplier_Eseye_with_an_adapter_board_for_evaluation_in_a_Mini-SIM_socket.jpg *License*: unknown *Contributors*: User:Paul Marshall UK

file:Thuraya sim.jpeg *Source*: http://en.wikipedia.org/w/index.php?title=File:Thuraya_sim.jpeg *License*: unknown *Contributors*: User:Towel401

file:Grameenphone SIM Both Side.JPG *Source*: http://en.wikipedia.org/w/index.php?title=File:Grameenphone_SIM_Both_Side.JPG *License*: unknown *Contributors*: User:Auyon

file:Au ic card.jpg *Source*: http://en.wikipedia.org/w/index.php?title=File:Au_ic_card.jpg *License*: unknown *Contributors*: U s e r :

file:NTT DoCoMo FOMA card chip green.jpg *Source*: http://en.wikipedia.org/w/index.php?title=File:NTT_DoCoMo_FOMA_card_chip_green.jpg *License*: unknown *Contributors*: User:Qurren

Image:Huawei E220 (Three).jpg *Source*: http://en.wikipedia.org/w/index.php?title=File:Huawei_E220_(Three).jpg *License*: unknown *Contributors*: User:Korax1214

GNU Free Documentation License Version 1.2, November 2002 Copyright (C) 2000,2001,2002 Free Software Foundation, Inc. 59 Temple Place, Suite 330, Boston, MA 02111-1307 USA Everyone is permitted to copy and distribute verbatim copies of this license document, but changing it is not allowed.

0. PREAMBLE

The purpose of this License is to make a manual, textbook, or other functional and useful document "free" in the sense of freedom: to assure everyone the effective freedom to copy and redistribute it, with or without modifying it, either commercially or noncommercially. Secondarily, this License preserves for the author and publisher a way to get credit for their work, while not being considered responsible for modifications made by others. This License is a kind of "copyleft", which means that derivative works of the document must themselves be free in the same sense. It complements the GNU General Public License, which is a copyleft license designed for free software. We have designed this License in order to use it for manuals for free software, because free software needs free documentation: a free program should come with manuals providing the same freedoms that the software does. But this License is not limited to software manuals; it can be used for any textual work, regardless of subject matter or whether it is published as a printed book. We recommend this License principally for works whose purpose is instruction or reference.

1. APPLICABILITY AND DEFINITIONS

This License applies to any manual or other work, in any medium, that contains a notice placed by the copyright holder saying it can be distributed under the terms of this License. Such a notice grants a world-wide, royalty-free license, unlimited in duration, to use that work under the conditions stated herein. The "Document", below, refers to any such manual or work. Any member of the public is a licensee, and is addressed as "you". You accept the license if you copy, modify or distribute the work in a way requiring permission under copyright law. A "Modified Version" of the Document means any work containing the Document or a portion of it, either copied verbatim, or with modifications and/or translated into another language. A "Secondary Section" is a named appendix or a front-matter section of the Document that deals exclusively with the relationship of the publishers or authors of the Document to the Document's overall subject (or to related matters) and contains nothing that could fall directly within that overall subject. (Thus, if the Document is in part a textbook of mathematics, a Secondary Section may not explain any mathematics.) The relationship could be a matter of historical connection with the subject or with related matters, or of legal, commercial, philosophical, ethical or political position regarding them. The "Invariant Sections" are certain Secondary Sections whose titles are designated, as being those of Invariant Sections, in the notice that says that the Document is released under this License. If a section does not fit the above definition of Secondary then it is not allowed to be designated as Invariant. The Document may contain zero Invariant Sections. If the Document does not identify any Invariant Sections then there are none. The "Cover Texts" are certain short passages of text that are listed, as Front-Cover Texts or Back-Cover Texts, in the notice that says that the Document is released under this License. A Front-Cover Text may be at most 5 words, and a Back-Cover Text may be at most 25 words. A "Transparent" copy of the Document means a machine-readable copy, represented in a format whose specification is available to the general public, that is suitable for revising the document straightforwardly with generic text editors or (for images composed of pixels) generic paint programs or (for drawings) some widely available drawing editor, and that is suitable for input to text formatters or for automatic translation to a variety of formats suitable for input to text formatters. A copy made in an otherwise Transparent file format whose markup, or absence of markup, has been arranged to thwart or discourage subsequent modification by readers is not Transparent. An image format is not Transparent if used for any substantial amount of text. A copy that is not "Transparent" is called "Opaque". Examples of suitable formats for Transparent copies include plain ASCII without markup, Texinfo input format, LaTeX input format, SGML or XML using a publicly available DTD, and standard-conforming simple HTML, PostScript or PDF designed for human modification. Examples of transparent image formats include PNG, XCF and JPG. Opaque formats include proprietary formats that can be read and edited only by proprietary word processors, SGML or XML for which the DTD and/or processing tools are not generally available, and the machine-generated HTML, PostScript or PDF produced by some word processors for output purposes only. The "Title Page" means, for a printed book, the title page itself, plus such following pages as are needed to hold, legibly, the material this License requires to appear in the title page. For works in formats which do not have any title page as such, "Title Page" means the text near the most prominent appearance of the work's title, preceding the beginning of the body of the text. A section "Entitled XYZ" means a named subunit of the Document whose title either is precisely XYZ or contains XYZ in parentheses following text that translates XYZ in another language. (Here XYZ stands for a specific section name mentioned below, such as "Acknowledgements", "Dedications", "Endorsements", or "History".) To "Preserve the Title" of such a section when you modify the Document means that it remains a section "Entitled XYZ" according to this definition. The Document may include Warranty Disclaimers next to the notice which states that this License applies to the Document. These Warranty Disclaimers are considered to be included by reference in this License, but only as regards disclaiming warranties: any other implication that these Warranty Disclaimers may have is void and has no effect on the meaning of this License.

2. VERBATIM COPYING

You may copy and distribute the Document in any medium, either commercially or noncommercially, provided that this License, the copyright notices, and the license notice saying this License applies to the Document are reproduced in all copies, and that you add no other conditions whatsoever to those of this License. You may not use technical measures to obstruct or control the reading or further copying of the copies you make or distribute. However, you may accept compensation in exchange for copies. If you distribute a large enough number of copies you must also follow the conditions in section 3. You may also lend copies, under the same conditions stated above, and you may publicly display copies.

3. COPYING IN QUANTITY

If you publish printed copies (or copies in media that commonly have printed covers) of the Document, numbering more than 100, and the Document's license notice requires Cover Texts, you must enclose the copies in covers that carry, clearly and legibly, all these Cover Texts: Front-Cover Texts on the front cover, and Back-Cover Texts on the back cover. Both covers must also clearly and legibly identify you as the publisher of these copies. The front cover must present the full title with all words of the title equally prominent and visible. You may add other material on the covers in addition. Copying with changes limited to the covers, as long as they preserve the title of the Document and satisfy these conditions, can be treated as verbatim copying in other respects. If the required texts for either cover are too voluminous to fit legibly, you should put the first ones listed (as many as fit reasonably) on the actual cover, and continue the rest onto adjacent pages. If you publish or distribute Opaque copies of the Document numbering more than 100, you must either include a machine-readable Transparent copy along with each Opaque copy, or state in or with each Opaque copy a computer-network location from which the general network-using public has access to download using public-standard network protocols a complete Transparent copy of the Document, free of added material. If you use the latter option, you must take reasonably prudent steps, when you begin distribution of Opaque copies in quantity, to ensure that this Transparent copy will remain thus accessible at the stated location until at least one year after the last time you distribute an Opaque copy (directly or through your agents or retailers) of that edition to the public. It is requested, but not required, that you contact the authors of the Document well before redistributing any large number of copies, to give them a chance to provide you with an updated version of the Document.

4. MODIFICATIONS

You may copy and distribute a Modified Version of the Document under the conditions of sections 2 and 3 above, provided that you release the Modified Version under precisely this License, with the Modified Version filling the role of the Document, thus licensing distribution and modification of the Modified Version to whoever possesses a copy of it. In addition, you must do these things in the Modified Version: A. Use in the Title Page (and on the covers, if any) a title distinct from that of the Document, and from those of previous versions (which should, if there were any, be listed in the History section of the Document). You may use the same title as a previous version if the original publisher of that version gives permission. B. List on the Title Page, as authors, one or more persons or entities responsible for authorship of the modifications in the Modified Version, together with at least five of the principal authors of the Document (all of its principal authors, if it has fewer than five), unless they release you from this requirement. C. State on the Title page the name of the publisher of the Modified Version, as the publisher. D. Preserve all the copyright notices of the Document. E. Add an appropriate copyright notice for your modifications adjacent to the other copyright notices. F. Include, immediately after the copyright notices, a license notice giving the public permission to use the Modified Version under the terms of this License, in the form shown in the Addendum below. G. Preserve in that license notice the full lists of Invariant Sections and required Cover Texts given in the Document's license notice. H. Include an unaltered copy of this License. I. Preserve the section Entitled "History", Preserve its Title, and add to it an item stating at least the title, year, new authors, and publisher of the Modified Version as given on the Title Page. If there is no section Entitled "History" in the Document, create one stating the title, year, authors, and publisher of the Document as given on its Title Page, then add an item describing the Modified Version as stated in the previous sentence. J. Preserve the network location, if any, given in the Document for public access to a Transparent copy of the Document, and likewise the network locations given in the Document for previous versions it was based on. These may be placed in the "History" section. You may omit a network location for a work that was published at least four years before the Document itself, or if the original publisher of the version it refers to gives permission. K. For any section Entitled "Acknowledgements" or "Dedications", Preserve the Title of the section, and preserve in the section all the substance and tone of each of the contributor acknowledgements and/or dedications given therein. L. Preserve all the Invariant Sections of the Document, unaltered in their text and in their titles. Section numbers or the equivalent are not considered part of the section titles. M. Delete any section Entitled "Endorsements". Such a section may not be included in the Modified Version. N. Do not retitle any existing section to be Entitled "Endorsements" or to conflict in title with any Invariant Section. O. Preserve any Warranty Disclaimers. If the Modified Version includes new front-matter sections or appendices that qualify as Secondary Sections and contain no material copied from the Document, you may at your option designate some or all of these sections as invariant. To do this, add their titles to the list of Invariant Sections in the Modified Version's license notice. These titles must be distinct from any other section titles. You may add a section Entitled "Endorsements", provided it contains nothing but endorsements of your Modified Version by various parties--for example, statements of peer review or that the text has been approved by an organization as the authoritative definition of a standard. You may add a passage of up to five words as a Front-Cover Text, and a passage of up to 25 words as a Back-Cover Text, to the end of the list of Cover Texts in the Modified Version. Only one passage of Front-Cover Text and one of Back-Cover Text may be added by (or through arrangements made by) any one entity. If the Document already includes a cover text for the same cover, previously added by you or by arrangement made by the same entity you are acting on behalf of, you may not add another; but you may replace the old one, on explicit permission from the previous publisher that added the old one. The author(s) and publisher(s) of the Document do not by this License give permission to use their names for publicity for or to assert or imply endorsement of any Modified Version.

5. COMBINING DOCUMENTS

You may combine the Document with other documents released under this License, under the terms defined in section 4 above for modified versions, provided that you include in the combination all of the Invariant Sections of all of the original documents, unmodified, and list them all as Invariant Sections of your combined work in its license notice, and that you preserve all their Warranty Disclaimers. The combined work need only contain one copy of this License, and multiple identical Invariant Sections may be replaced with a single copy. If there are multiple Invariant Sections with the same name but different contents, make the title of each such section unique by adding at the end of it, in parentheses, the name of the original author or publisher of that section if known, or else a unique number. Make the same adjustment to the section titles in the list of Invariant Sections in the license notice of the combined work. In the combination, you must combine any sections Entitled "History" in the various original documents, forming one section Entitled "History"; likewise combine any sections Entitled "Acknowledgements", and any sections Entitled "Dedications". You must delete all sections Entitled "Endorsements".

6. COLLECTIONS OF DOCUMENTS

You may make a collection consisting of the Document and other documents released under this License, and replace the individual copies of this License in the various documents with a single copy that is included in the collection, provided that you follow the rules of this License for verbatim copying of each of the documents in all other respects. You may extract a single document from such a collection, and distribute it individually under this License, provided you insert a copy of this License into the extracted document, and follow this License in all other respects regarding verbatim copying of that document.

7. AGGREGATION WITH INDEPENDENT WORKS

A compilation of the Document or its derivatives with other separate and independent documents or works, in or on a volume of a storage or distribution medium, is called an "aggregate" if the copyright resulting from the compilation is not used to limit the legal rights of the compilation's users beyond what the individual works permit. When the Document is included in an aggregate, this License does not apply to the other works in the aggregate which are not themselves derivative works of the Document. If the Cover Text requirement of section 3 is applicable to these copies of the Document, then if the Document is less than one half of the entire aggregate, the Document's Cover Texts may be placed on covers that bracket the Document within the aggregate, or the electronic equivalent of covers if the Document is in electronic form. Otherwise they must appear on printed covers that bracket the whole aggregate.

8. TRANSLATION

Translation is considered a kind of modification, so you may distribute translations of the Document under the terms of section 4. Replacing Invariant Sections with translations requires special permission from their copyright holders, but you may include translations of some or all Invariant Sections in addition to the original versions of these Invariant Sections. You may include a translation of this License, and all the license notices in the Document, and any Warranty Disclaimers, provided that you also include the original English version of this License and the original versions of those notices and disclaimers. In case of a disagreement between the translation and the original version of this License or a notice or disclaimer, the original version will prevail. If a section in the Document is Entitled "Acknowledgements", "Dedications", or "History", the requirement (section 4) to Preserve its Title (section 1) will typically require changing the actual title.

9. TERMINATION

You may not copy, modify, sublicense, or distribute the Document except as expressly provided for under this License. Any other attempt to copy, modify, sublicense or distribute the Document is void, and will automatically terminate your rights under this License. However, parties who have received copies, or rights, from you under this License will not have their licenses terminated so long as such parties remain in full compliance.

10. FUTURE REVISIONS OF THIS LICENSE

The Free Software Foundation may publish new, revised versions of the GNU Free Documentation License from time to time. Such new versions will be similar in spirit to the present version, but may differ in detail to address new problems or concerns. See http://www.gnu.org/copyleft/. Each version of the License is given a distinguishing version number. If the Document specifies that a particular numbered version of this License "or any later version" applies to it, you have the option of following the terms and conditions either of that specified version or of any later version that has been published (not as a draft) by the Free Software Foundation. If the Document does not specify a version number of this License, you may choose any version ever published (not as a draft) by the Free Software Foundation. ADDENDUM: How to use this License for your documents To use this License in a document you have written, include a copy of the License in the document and put the following copyright and license notices just after the title page: Copyright (c) YEAR YOUR NAME. Permission is granted to copy, distribute and/or modify this document under the terms of the GNU Free Documentation License, Version 1.2 or any later version published by the Free Software Foundation; with no Invariant Sections, no Front-Cover Texts, and no Back-Cover Texts. A copy of the license is included in the section entitled "GNU Free Documentation License". If you have Invariant Sections, Front-Cover Texts and Back-Cover Texts, replace the "with...Texts." line with this: with the Invariant Sections being LIST THEIR TITLES, with the Front-Cover Texts being LIST, and with the Back-Cover Texts being LIST. If you have Invariant Sections without Cover Texts, or some other combination of the three, merge those two alternatives to suit the situation. If your document contains nontrivial examples of program code, we recommend releasing these examples in parallel under your choice of free software license, such as the GNU General Public License, to permit their use in free software.